AMERICAN CULTURE
AND
CATHOLIC SCHOOLS

BY EMMETT MCLOUGHLIN

PEOPLE'S PADRE

AMERICAN CULTURE
and
CATHOLIC SCHOOLS

by

Emmett McLoughlin

LYLE STUART · NEW YORK

Printed in the United States of America

Contents

DEDICATION

To my wife, Mary, who has been a comforter and advisor in the troubles and problems of the last eleven years and a companion in their joys and successes.

AMERICAN CULTURE
AND
CATHOLIC SCHOOLS

Introduction

The political strength of the Catholic Church in America lies in the carefully developed and constantly repeated illusion of great numerical strength. A natural, and to the Catholic hierarchy, a desired corollary to this numerical strength, is great voting strength and great financial strength. The voting strength could elect or defeat friendly or unfriendly candidates. The financial strength could promote or destroy friendly or unfriendly companies, magazines, newspapers or radio and television stations.

This illusion of numbers is responsible for the great fear that exists among non-Catholic politicians and businessmen.

The core of this strength is the united hierarchy and the indoctrinated minority of the laity, who are the "shock troops" of the Church. They are the unthinking, obedient, docile Catholics who refuse to read condemned books, who vote for Catholic candidates, who do the Church's bidding when they get onto school boards, library boards or city commissions. The training of this very effective and well disciplined "Church militant" in America is the successful function and accomplishment of the Roman Catholic parochial school system.

I feel that the majority of Catholic children who pass through the parochial school system shake off its mental strait jacket, as they rub elbows physically and mentally with other Americans in business, politics and marriage. These Catholics whom the parochial school system does not succeed in indoctrinating seem to fall into three groups.

The first we might call "liberal" Catholics. They preserve the external formality of Catholicism, such as attendance at Mass and occasional communion. However, they do not let the hierarchy influence them. They think as they please, vote as they please and live as they please, particularly as concerns birth control.

The second group comprise the vast numbers of those who give up the practice of their religion entirely, with the occasional exception of the Easter service or the Christmas midnight Mass. They, too, vote as they please. They marry and divorce at will, condemn the clergy for its narrow-mindedness or its attempts to interfere with their personal and private lives. But they are too mentally indolent to drop the name "Catholic." When they go to a hospital, they pick a non-Catholic hospital so that, even though they list their religion as Catholic, they will not be pestered by a priest.

The third group of the "disappointing" products of the parochial school system are the ex-Catholics. They are the army of those who have thought their way through and have become disillusioned with the Church—its religious doctrine, its lack of true religion, its mental tyranny, its history of mental and physical oppression throughout the centuries, and its present-day, world-wide grasping for religious, political and financial power.

These ex-Catholics are vocal. They are concerned that the Church's history of medieval control or the examples of modern Spain and Latin America (aggravated by the default of Protestants) may be repeated in America. Ex-Catholics are extremely impatient with the "tolerance" and complacency of the majority of Protestants. They scorn Protestants who are afraid of offending Catholics and their clergy, even in areas such as New England where the vocal, closely-knit Catholic minority has already taken over public school boards, city commissions and even state governments.

No one knows how many ex-Catholics who attended Catholic schools there are in America; but there must be a very large number. I have received a constant stream of letters from them in the decade since I left the Roman priesthood and, particularly, since the publication of my book, *People's Padre*. I have met thousands of ex-Catholics during my lecture tours across the country.

In spite of the large majority of American Catholic children on whom the hierarchy's efforts are wasted, still the parochial school is the principal weapon in the Church's campaign to "make America Catholic"—to control the nation through censorship, politics and religion. It needs only a minority of intensely indoctrinated devotees to man the many control fronts of press, radio, television, public school boards, teaching staffs, community efforts, city commissions, state legislatures and even the Congress of the United States.

The parochial schools are cut off from the freedom of thought of the public schools. This isolation enables them to indoctrinate those who yield to them with an intensity approaching that of a seminary or a convent. It alone can produce the necessary quantity of the "party workers" or "shock troopers" who believe that there is a soul-saving martyrdom in dying for God and Holy Mother Church. They remain totally oblivious to the fact that, when they are martyred, it is not for religion or God at all; but because they have been pawns in some scheme of the hierarchy to take over or continue the political control of a country. It alone can so condition them that, whenever non-Catholics object to some encroachment on their civil liberties, even in America, Catholic shock troopers with their priests will scream that this non-Catholic self-defense is an attack on God. They brand it a manifestation of the "gates of hell" fighting the one true Church. They proclaim that any and all critics of anything the hierarchy does or says are anti-Catholic, bigots and persecutors.

The parochial school alone, with constant religious services in big churches, can instill into this dedicated minority the concept of the bigness of Catholicism. So it makes them unafraid to assert themselves as representatives of vast thousands of people with the influence of an irresistible voting block or financial power. An absurdly small number of them will appear in order to high pressure a city ordinance on "obscene" literature or threaten to break up the United Fund if it admits the Planned Parenthood Foundation. The Catholic parochial school system trains this minority to make so much noise in America that they create the illusion of numbers and power. This clamor frightens the non-Catholics of the country. The real power of the American Catholic hierarchy is the fear in the minds of non-Catholics.

Throughout this book, when I point out the effectiveness of the Catholic parochial school, with its supporting media of Catholic ritual, Catholic press, censorship, etc., I refer to the effectiveness of Catholic indoctrination on the *minority* of its own people. There are more than four million children in Catholic schools. It is probably generous to estimate that its system is lastingly effective as to doctrine and loyalty on only one-third of these children. That represents only about one million four hundred thousand Americans who are being thoroughly indoctrinated in a system of thought completely at variance with the American concept of political and, especially, mental liberty.

But, if we had an American school system successfully indoctrinating one million four hundred thousand American Communist children out of four million, we would certainly be seriously concerned.

I was trained as one of the "shock troops" of the Roman Catholic Church.

CHAPTER ONE

The Well-Washed Brain

I am a product of the Roman Catholic educational system in America. I attended St. Francis parochial grammar school in Sacramento, California, and, for two years, the Christian Brothers College (high school) in that same city. For twelve subsequent years (1922-1934) I was enrolled in the junior and senior seminaries of the Franciscan Order in Santa Barbara, California.

As a Catholic priest for fifteen years, I was also a teacher in the Roman Catholic educational system. I taught in St. Mary's Grammar and Girls' High School and St. Joseph's School of Nursing—all in Phoenix, Arizona.

In the years since I left the Roman Church and its priesthood in 1948, I have constantly been attempting to evaluate the education that I received, both in and out of the classroom, from the Roman Catholic Church. I have been curious as to whether my training was typical of Catholic education throughout the country. I wanted to know how it compared with the public educational system which I had not been permitted even to sample.

Since leaving the priesthood, I have received thousands of letters from ex-Catholics. Invariably they write of their school days in the Catholic parochial system. They are always bitter about those days. One man told of running away from a seminary eleven times before his parents would allow him to attend an art school.

There are infinitely more ex-Catholics than Rome knows of or would care to admit. Their apparent unanimity of feeling endorsing my own uneasiness about the value of my Catholic education has prompted the study which has resulted in this book. The gathering of material, the searching of libraries in New York, Boston, Chicago, Kansas City, Los Angeles and other cities while lecturing across the country, the writing and re-writing, and considering the well-meaning, but sometimes devastating, comments of critics have taken approximately five years of my spare time from the administration of Memorial Hospital in Phoenix.

No doubt my having been a Catholic priest will cause Catholic critics to brand this book as biased and prejudiced. I have made every effort to be objective. I have purchased a complete library of Latin texts—moral and dogmatic theology, and canon law and more Catholic grammar and high school textbooks than I ever saw as a student.

My Catholic library is so well known that a Catholic neighbor sent his son, who wishes to become a priest, to me to borrow some books to prepare his term paper on "The Last Judgment" for St. Mary's Boys' High School. (Among other books I offered the boy was the Standard Revised version of the Bible and I suggested that he close his paper with the Gospel description of the Last

Judgment. He refused the Bible because it was not a Catholic Bible, but said he would use his own. His father later told me that the family had no Bible at all.)

The Roman Catholic educational system enrolls four million American young people and graduates about three hundred thousand annually to take their places beside their non-Catholic companions in this democracy. The Roman Catholic bishops have demanded that their educational system be given equal treatment with that of the American public schools. Clearly this means the support of public funds for Roman Catholic education.

Obviously this question becomes a crucial public issue. Perhaps public support of parochial education is what America wants. Perhaps America wishes to support Lutheran, Methodist, Congregational, Unitarian and other educational institutions as well. As it happens, only the Catholic leaders have requested such support, however, and therefore the focus of attention is upon the Catholic educational system.

What is the nature and purpose of Roman Catholic education? What are its methods and results? What effects will such education have on democratic institutions, and what impact will such a system exert upon the traditional American way of life?

In view of the demand of the Catholic bishops, America has a right to ask these questions before opening the public treasury. And America has a right to frank, honest, objective, documented answers.

The fact is that there has never been published a thoroughgoing objective study of the Roman Catholic educational system. No such answers are available in any book now in print, so far as we know. Hence *this* book.

In other words, this book is issued in the public welfare. It has no other purpose than to provide necessary information in an area of critical public decision where the information has not been previously available.

The average Protestant American knows little of the Roman Catholic school system. He passes St. Anthony's or the Immaculate Conception on his way to work. He sees nuns herding the youngsters around the school yard and wonders how they can control childish mischief when their veils hamper their vision like blinkers on a horse. He reads in his sports page that in boxing the Sacred Heart has knocked the whey out of the Holy Trinity, in football All Saints have romped all over the Holy Spirit, and in track St. Joseph has out-run Our Lady of the Angels.

However, this medieval anachronism becomes a very real threat when his son announces that he is in love with a Catholic girl, that he intends to marry her and that he is ready to sign a promise that his unborn children will be trained in Catholic schools.

The aim of the Catholic school is to train Catholics. Everything else is subordinate to this primary goal. The American parochial school that I attended was not an institution in which American children were drilled in reading, writing, arithmetic, spelling, geography and a class a day in the Catholic religion. It was a school in which we lived the Catholic Church. We lived within its aura and in its reflected light. We picked up as incidentals the subjects that Americans usually identify as the essence of an educational system. These subjects were important—but not primary.

This is not a prejudiced statement. Pope Pius XI in his encyclical on the Christian education of youth states:

The right of the Catholic Church and the family are not safeguarded merely by having the doctrine of (Catholic) religion taught in schools as a class (it is generally done sketchily) even by *Catholic* teachers. To have these rights satisfied in a school, it is necessary that all instruction and doctrine, the entire organization of the school,—teachers, curriculum, textbooks, the atmosphere of discipline—must be so saturated with and exude the Catholic spirit, under the rule and maternal vigilance of the Catholic Church, that the Catholic religion itself shall be the foundation and the crown of all education. This perspective shall obtain, not only in elementary schools but in higher schools as well. "For it is necessary," if we may use the words of Leo XIII (Enc. *Militantis Ecclesiae*, August 1, 1897), "not only at certain hours to teach Catholic religion to children but that all other subjects must also be made fragrant with the odor of piety. If this be not done, if this holy habit should not pervade and permeate the souls of both teachers and pupils, little benefit will accrue from any teaching but generally very great harm." [1]

Leo Pfeffer in *Church, State, and Freedom* condenses that encyclical into one paragraph:

These words of Pius XI epitomize the whole Catholic philosophy of education and the educational foundation of the Catholic parochial school system. Catholic doctrine does not conceive of religion as a subject which, like history or music, can be taught more or less independently of other subjects a specified number of school hours weekly; in the Catholic school religion is not merely a branch in the curriculum, nor is it confined to mere instruction. The ultimate goal of education is the praise, reverence and service of God; and everything else in education must be subordinated and directed toward this ulimate end. [2]

This all-pervading Catholicism is brought down from

papal encyclicals and textbooks to the point where "we must guide the child in acquiring the right values along with his arithmetic and grammar." [3]

And again: "All experience indicates that educators must work very hard and not flag for a single day if the job of making Christian piety permeate every school subject is to be accomplished." [4]

Msgr. Thomas J. Quigley, the Superintendent of the Schools of the Diocese of Pittsburgh, spelled out this application: "I do not believe the (Catholic) doctrine class should be cluttered up with Bible or church history. These belong to the history class. Church music belongs in the music class, study of the rubrics (ceremonies of worship) belongs in the art class. This, it seems to me, is the way to Catholicize the curriculum, not by bringing every other area of social inheritance into the Christian doctrine class, but by bringing the Christian (Catholic) inheritance into every other class in the curriculum." [5]

The writings of some priests on the necessity of the Catholic parochial school do not stop with an *implied* condemnation of the public school. They become very explicit: "Our first duty to the public school is not to pay taxes for its maintenance . . . Justice cannot oblige the support of a system which we are forbidden in conscience to use, or a system which we conscientiously hold to be bad in principle and bad in its ultimate consequences . . . The first duty of every Catholic father to the public school is to keep his children out of it. The first duty of every Catholic American to education in general is to support the Catholic school." (Fr. Paul Blakely, S. J., quoted in *Educational Forum,* November, 1954, p. 72.)

Fr. Blakely was no over-enthusiastic clerical maverick. He was echoing Pope Pius XII, who in his encyclical *Sertum Laetitiae* said: "We raise our voice in strong, albeit paternal complaint that in so many schools of your land Christ is often despised or ignored . . . and new educational systems are sought after which cannot but produce a sorrowful harvest in the intellectual and moral life of the nation." [6]

A living exemplar of Msgr. Quigley's ideal was the parochial school, St. Francis, on 26th and K Streets in Sacramento, California, in which I was enrolled at the age of six in September of 1913. The extension of that Catholic atmosphere was the overall theme of St. Francis school.

I believe it is less painful for Catholic youngsters to begin school in a Catholic school than for Protestant children to be thrown into the strange new world of a public school.

The Catholic grammar school is always adjacent to the parish church. When I was about the age of three, my parents started taking me to Sunday Mass. Long before school age, I was already familiar with my future teachers, the priests and the nuns, with the church building, the school grounds and the neighborhood.

My home environment led right into the Catholic school. Crucifixes were on the wall, as were pictures of Christ, Mary and the saints. Meat was never eaten on Friday. Most of my parents' friends were Irish Catholics and conversation frequently revolved about the Church and their children in the parochial school. They were in the American world, but certainly not of it. The atmosphere in which I moved as a pre-school child was thor-

oughly Roman Catholic. Any childish variation, doubt
or question was impossible and unthinkable.

As students, we saw only the brown-robed Franciscan
nuns and the Franciscan priests. We were very strongly
urged to arrive in time every morning to attend the eight
o'clock Mass in the old church adjoining the school. The
formal indoctrination in Catholicism took place every day
in the catechism and "Bible history" classes. The informal
indoctrination went on all day long. Catholic prayers were
recited in common at the beginning and end of every class
period. The crucifix occupied the most prominent wall in
every classroom and corridor. It was flanked by pictures
of Mary and a saint, usually St. Joseph or St. Anthony.
In the corner of almost every classroom was a little altar,
dedicated to Mary, with her statue and the flickering red
of the votive candle before it. We were encouraged to
bring flowers from our home gardens to place before Our
Lady.

All subjects were taught with a Catholic flavor. The
Benziger "readers" drilled us in English, as they taught us
the stories of the medieval Church. Even the geography
textbooks embellished the descriptions of the New World
with tales of the brave explorations of the "sons of the
Church."

Bible history is artfully substituted for the Bible itself.
The excuse for the substitution is that the Bible is too
long to cover in the classroom, that too many sections are
beyond the pupils' comprehension. Moreover, since Christ
appointed the Church as His interpreter, it is perfectly
logical for the hierarchy to select those passages and incidents of Holy Writ that are within the ken of its children

and will provide the greatest spiritual inspiration without causing any religious doubts.

Never once, in all the years that I attended a parochial grammar school and high school, can I recall a priest or a nun or a teaching Christian Brother using the Bible itself to prove a point of Catholic doctrine in a religion class or to emphasize a matter of behavior in an exhortation to the student body—or in prayer. The incontrovertible authority was simply, "The Church says so."

Nor, in fact, can I remember the Bible being used in class or our being encouraged to probe it privately during the five junior years in St. Anthony's Seminary in Santa Barbara. When we began our four-year course in theology, eight years after we had entered the seminary (seventeen years after I had begun my Catholic education) we were given a Catholic Bible. We were told that we were expected to read it through once during the next four years. This was to provide a background for our theological course in Exegesis—the interpretation of the Scriptures according to Catholic tradition.

During the last seven years of our studies for the Catholic priesthood, "spiritual reading" was an obligation for us. It was done publicly during our meals in the monastery refectory and we were expected to do it privately in our cells. The monastery library was filled with the lives of the saints and the treatises of ascetic writers. Neither during all those years of training nor in the fifteen years that I was a Roman Catholic priest was it ever suggested that as "spiritual reading" I might try the Bible.

But back to St. Francis Grammar School. In the main, the same curriculum was taught in our parochial school that the children in the neighboring public schools were taught—arithmetic, penmanship, geography, spelling, history, etc. We never had a course in hygiene.

In high school, too, the Christian Brothers were under the indirect pressure of the public school system because of the interchange of students and the admission standards of the junior colleges and the state universities. Again the curriculum—algebra, geometry, languages, etc.—was the same as in public schools. However, even in these years, the principal subject was the Catholic religion; and the principal loyalty instilled was to the Catholic Church and its leaders.

We were likewise taught that we were Americans. We were not taught what being an American means or what its principles are. The native Irish clergy, however, never missed an opportunity of reminding us of our misfortune in having been born in America and not in Ireland.

In the parochial schools that I attended, there was no thought of argument in the teaching of Catholicism. The old phrase of history forbade it—"Roma locuta, causa finita." ("Rome has spoken, the matter is settled.") No independence of thought was tolerated. We were taught that our priest would do the thinking for us in all matters of religion—or anything connected with religion. (A psychiatrist friend has told me the major difficulty in treating devout Catholics is that it is impossible to reach them. They don't think for themselves, he said, and the priest won't come with the patient to share in the treatment.)

This prohibition of thought made everything pertaining to our souls and our eternal future easy. We merely learned the catechism by rote and repeated in unison over and over the simple answers of the catechism day after day. In those days, a doubt regarding the Church's doctrine, its morals, its rituals, or its activities, political or otherwise, in American life, never occurred to me.

For me, in my early childhood, no lasting organization existed but the Roman Catholic Church. When I was a very small child, my mother instilled into me two concepts: the greatness of the Irish and the greatness of the Roman Catholic Church. The two were inseparable and for years I thrilled on St. Patrick's day to the sermons of Irish priests who identified the two as the greatest and most lasting combination in the history of humanity.

As a boy, I had no recreation outside of the Roman Catholic Church. My parents permitted me to join a Boy Scout troop, but it had to be a Catholic Boy Scout troop. Its meetings were held in St. Francis School. Its leader was a Roman Catholic priest. Its summer encampment was always under the auspices of the Catholic Church and the daily program started with Mass every morning.

My most frequent contact with non-Catholics was my boyhood work of delivering newspapers for the Sacramento BEE. I met boys who were not Catholic; but still there was always the reserve and the feeling that these were not my people nor God's people, that I merely had to tolerate them in order to earn the money for delivering newspapers.

Our home life throughout my grammar school days was Catholic life. We observed all the rules of the Roman Catholic Church regarding fasting in Lent, abstinence from meat on Friday and attendance at Mass, not only on Sunday, but on every holy day. I can remember, when delivering morning papers of the San Francisco EXAM-

INER, of dropping the sack of papers behind the rear pew in St. Francis' church while I attended Mass. Missing Mass on Sunday was absolutely unthinkable.

I was so loyal and dutiful that I was made an altar boy and considered it a tremendous honor to assist at Mass within the altar railing, to offer the priest the wine and water and to ring the bell at the sacred part of the ceremony. I received prizes for my attendance in serving Mass and proudly wore the St. Christopher medal and the miraculous medal of the Virgin Mary. I felt that I was one of the most honored boys on earth and that what I was doing would be rewarded in eternity. I believed that I enjoyed a privilege far beyond anything that could be done for me by the City of Sacramento or the United States of America.

As a youngster, I had no doubts about the Catholic Church. How could I? Its voice was the voice of God reaching back across the centuries and into eternity. Its voice carried the finality and assurance of God Himself.

In those young years of grammar school, I was being hopefully trained to be one of the "Church militant"—a "shock trooper" in the hierarchy's desire to expand itself, to carry "Christ's message of revelation," to "make America Catholic." In other words, my education was designed to help the Church become richer and its bishops more powerful.

The principal quality must be loyalty to the Church. The Church was a vague, distant thing; so I was taught that loyalty must be to the nuns and priests I could see. Later this must become obedience; still later, blind obedience. In the years at the seminary, the example was given that we should be as obedient as a dead body which always stayed where it was placed. A recent book praising the Jesuits is entitled *The Obedient Men.*

One of the great paradoxes of American life is that the American Catholic child is brought up in the land of Thomas Jefferson, Benjamin Franklin and Abraham Lincoln (with their heritage of freedom of thought and complete mental liberty) still adhering to a school system and a rigidity of thought reminiscent of the Middle Ages and its mental tyranny.

Why does the Catholic parochial school system succeed even as well as it does? It is understandable that a majority of these youngsters, mingling after school hours with other American children who are not Roman Catholic—and particularly when passing through adolescence— lose the intensity of their loyalty to the Catholic system. As I have said before, probably two-thirds of Catholic children, even though brought up in the parochial school system, become liberal or lukewarm or abandon Catholicism altogether. The remarkable thing is that even the minority remains so fanatically faithful and devoted.

I think that the secret of the Catholic school system's success with those it does indoctrinate lies in its identification with God. As little children, we were taught that the voice of the Church was the voice of God. This was the constant emphasis. The Church was established by the God-Christ. It could do no wrong. It could say no wrong. Its pronouncements were the decrees of God. To us little children, the nuns and the priests represented the authority not of a school, certainly not of a city or of a state, but the authority of God Himself.

In belonging to this group we belonged to the vastest group in the universe. We were not merely citizens of a

very recent nation, the United States. Far more important, we were united to the Church and with the Church
to Christ and through Christ, by direct lineage, to David,
Solomon, Moses, to Adam and the infinite eternity of God
Himself. There was now eternity of relationship behind
us and an eternity of happiness ahead of us, an eternity
which we could reach only through obedience, loyalty
and faith to the Roman Catholic Church, the only voice
and authority of God on earth and, in time, the certainty
of that eternity ahead.

I believe that all Catholic children in the Catholic
school are imbued with an intense feeling of loyalty. I
believe that a majority of them know this after they get
out of school and particularly after they marry. There is
an initial emotion that is undoubtedly not felt by children
in the public school.

In St. Francis School in Sacramento, California, we
felt that, although we constituted only a few hundred
children in comparison to the many thousands in the public school system, we belonged to an organization far
more vast than the children in the public schools. We
might be a minority here in Sacramento; but around the
world we were the biggest church, much bigger than the
United States of America. We were the main church in
Italy, France, Spain and all Mexico and the South American countries. In all those countries we had more people
than there were Protestants in the *whole world*.

Furthermore, the Protestants, and we were taught this
as little children, were only a few years old. They started
with a sinful priest by the name of Martin Luther, who
finally threw an ink bottle at the devil to soothe his con-

science, and by Henry VIII, who murdered a succession of wives in a vain attempt to find happiness outside the Catholic Church.

But all the great heroes of history, we were taught, were on our side—and that included St. Francis School—Columbus, the explorers of the Western hemisphere, the early scientists, the monks who preserved learning, the Popes who civilized the Goths and the Visigoths, the Popes who outlasted Rome, Peter the Rock whom Jesus chose, Christ Himself, and through Him all the sincere Jews back to Abraham and again through Adam to the Holy Trinity itself and all the angels of Heaven. All were on our side and on our side alone. We were all of one family.

From St. Francis School in Sacramento back through thousands of years and on into eternity, I was part of the vastest assembly ever to exist. Compared to this, the whole United States and all of its Protestants were a recent flash in the pan of time. All of this greatness in numbers around the world, this authority of a church spanning all human history, the awesomeness of the uncountable host of angels and the power of God Himself constituted a force that no one boy could resist. What the Church taught must be true. What the Church decreed I must obey. This, I think, is the heart of the secret of why the Catholic educational system can elicit the loyalty it does from the youngsters who surrender with full mind and heart to its tremendous emotional appeal.

The Catholic school is the voice of the Catholic Church. The Catholic Church was the only voice of God and it alone was unwavering and unassailable truth. Any criticism of it was an attack of the devil. Any teaching contrary to it had to be false without even being examined or questioned.

This was the feeling that grew stronger as the years went by in my progress through a Catholic school. The study of history or arithmetic or dramatics or singing was as much a part of the Catholic religion as hearing Mass or going to confession or receiving communion. The school and the Church were on the same property and part of the same system. We went to Mass and then to class and then to confession (in a body) and then back to class.

The history textbook would tell of the Catholic civilization of Europe. Then we would celebrate St. Patrick's Day on March 17th and the glory of the Irish, who were the main civilizers, we were taught, of America. Then we would go back to class on March 18th. Then on March 19th we celebrated the feast of St. Joseph, the foster father of Jesus Christ, and all day long we would hear the praise of this foster father of Jesus and the chaste protector of Mary. On the 20th, we would be back again in arithmetic and Catholic history.

Another difference between our school and the neighboring public schools was that religious reasons were always sufficient for forgetting mundane studies.

Classes were always interrupted for a visit from the local bishop or a story by a passing missionary from the Orient. He would describe the poverty of the schools and churches and we would put our pennies in the boxes for buying babies for the Catholic orphanages.

We loved the toll of the church's funeral bells. A few of us were always excused from classes to "serve" the funeral Mass and accompany the priest to the cemetery to hold the holy water and the incense pot while he dolefully consigned "ashes to ashes and dust to dust." It was hard for us to appreciate the sadness of the occasion because marriages gave us the same break from classes.

The monthly communion on the "First Friday" of every month was a gala occasion. We came fasting and breakfast was served after Mass. This cut out several hours of classes. So did the confession period of the afternoon before.

We felt much luckier than public school pupils. We enjoyed not only the holidays of the country but were also excused from classes on the major holidays of the Church.

All of these non-classroom aspects of the parochial school only served, of course, to mold us more closely into the Church's concept of not merely educated youngsters but educated Catholics.

Throughout my boyhood, my idols and those of most of my schoolmates were the priests of the parish. They represented the Church and, through the Church, they represented God. In a vague way, we believed that all good boys should try to become priests. Perhaps the priesthood represented an aristocracy attainable to poor Irish children. We were taught that it was much more important than being a city commissioner, a mayor, a governor or a successful businessman.

In my case, I was torn between the desire to enter the priesthood and a need to go to work and help my father support our family. My father frequently told me that, as the oldest child, I should assume the responsibility of helping him support my brother and sisters.

However, the opposition of my parents to my entry

into the seminary was not dramatic or serious. Nor was there any aspect of defiance in my desire to go. They would have preferred for me to wait a few more years. My father received only a small salary to support a wife and four children and expressed the thought that my help after finishing high school might relieve the strain. I felt this obligation but had no idea of how to carry it out. There was no thought of my going to college. Among our Irish Catholic circle, only snobs went to college; and they usually lost their faith. My mother wanted to keep her first-born son near her as long as possible. She may have felt that she was losing her son. When I first left, she cried bitterly at the railroad station. Her first letters seemed filled with grief; but I was too young to appreciate her emotions.

I do not believe my parents would have dared openly and seriously to forbid me to study for the priesthood. They were too thoroughly saturated with Catholicism. The priest wished me to enter the seminary. To them, the wish of the priest was the wish of the Church. The wish of the Church was the wish of God. To defy the wish of God was sinful. It was that simple.

As with thousands of young American Catholics, the pressure to enter the seminary took place long before I was conscious of what a normal life might be or the desirability of companionship between boys and girls.

I was attending the Christian Brothers High School in Sacramento, after graduation from St. Francis Grammar School. Two of my classmates had gone into the seminary to study for the priesthood. They gave glowing accounts of the ocean, the mountains, and the pleasure of living in the seminary in Santa Barbara. I entered the seminary with the enthusiasm with which a boy might go on a picnic.

In a vague way, I was idealistic about offering my life to the service of God and of doing my part to save souls. The immediate inducement was the promise of picnics on the ocean and hikes into the mountains. Once I was in the seminary, the intensity of the indoctrination towards celibacy and the priesthood began.

I entered St. Anthony's Seminary in Santa Barbara in 1922. It would naturally be assumed that here great emphasis would be placed on religion. Curiously enough a much greater emphasis was placed on Latin. My "transcript of record" from the seminary high school department shows during the four years 1216 periods in Latin and 342 periods in Religion. The other subjects were English, Public Speaking, Greek, German, Spanish, History, Science (Algebra, Geometry, Physics) and Gregorian Chant. The Bible was not studied. Physics was a non-laboratory course that was remarkably unproductive.

The Senior Seminary, or "college" course, was simply a trade apprenticeship in priestly functions and indoctrination. We were taught "liberal arts" from the Catholic viewpoint, history only from the Catholic viewpoint, Catholic scholastic philosophy, and moral and dogmatic theology as handed down by the "fathers of the Church" and the "great theologians." The analysis or exegesis of the Scriptures is listed in my transcript under the subject "English" and is entitled "Literature of the Bible."

I spent twenty-one years in Catholic schools. I was told that they were as good as any Catholic schools in America. The nuns told my parents that I was a good student. They skipped me from the sixth to the eighth grade. In later collegiate years, I was considered a straight-A student.

In a contest during my first year in the Christian Brothers High School in Sacramento, I won the gold medal award for excellence in Catholic Doctrine. The medal later proved of great value. On the following St. Patrick's Day, while our family was attending the celebration of the Ancient Order of Hibernians, of which my father had been secretary for over twenty years, an astute robber ransacked our house. The police caught the man and found the loot buried on the side of the levee near the American River. The identifying article was my engraved Catholic Doctrine medal. We recovered our valuables.

Throughout my Catholic education, I was well grounded in subjects that could be learned by rote or practice. I achieved excellence in the Palmer method of penmanship. I did well in spelling bees. Arithmetic was easy till I reached logarithms. The nuns drilled me in geography until I knew the capital of every obscure land on earth. The history of America was hazy, but I knew that it was based on Catholic teachings. I also knew the date of every major event in the advance of Catholicism in Europe.

But I did not learn to think. As the years of childhood slipped through a frustrated adolescence (in the seminary) into the days that were supposed to be those of manhood, my mind was molded in an intellectual pattern as effectively as though it had been cast in concrete. The term "brain-washed" is applied to Chinese Communism, but the practice is as old as the Catholic school system.

The closest approach to science that I experienced in those twenty-one years was that non-laboratory course in elemental physics. Our education was so much in the past that it was reminiscent of the Arabic or Jewish schools of the Moorish and Hebraic days when the students clustered about the Rabbis and chanted aloud, as they fruitlessly committed to memory the ancient geneologies from King David back to Adam.

Of the world's really great literature, in twelve years I learned practically nothing. Its greatest lights were locked in the prison of the *Index of Forbidden Books.* John Ruskin's *Seven Lamps of Architecture* was available. I read it again and again and again. I was not interested in the backs of gargoyles, or flying buttresses or the pitch of a Gothic arch. But Ruskin's poetic prose taught me the use of the English tongue far better than the displaced German priests (some from the Franco-Prussian War) or sons of the German-American ghettos who tried to teach us the art of preaching in the so-called science of homiletics.

In short—I was not educated. I was merely indoctrinated. I had achieved the level of the rigor mortis of intellectual mediocrity.

I had become an automaton, a priest of sacred, half-known rites as meaningless in their efficacy as the chants of a Puerto Rican voodoo priest or the blessings of Tibet's sacred Lama.

I was an ecclesiastical technician trained to mold other young, pliable minds and change their mental blood stream as effectively as our hospital's doctors and technicians change the body of a newborn baby whose blood is Rh negative. I was trained to teach growing youngsters that voting and saluting were the essence of Americanism, while I was also teaching them the principles that would destroy democracy. I was teaching them, in the days of St. Monica's Church, that it was honorable and sacred to fight and to die that democracy might live; while their and my hierarchy was planning that democracy, as we knew and loved it, must die.

I was a dedicated soldier of the "Church militant"—an indoctrinated "shock trooper."

CHAPTER TWO

Education by Edict

It is obvious that the observations in the previous chapter constitute a strong indictment of that segment of the Roman Catholic school system with which I came in personal association.

When I left the priesthood and found that state universities would not acknowledge my seminary credits as worthy of even a bachelor's degree, I thought that perhaps my Catholic schools and teachers had been exceptionally inferior and not typical of the Catholic school system as a whole.

I determined to find out if this were true and made a thoroughgoing study of the entire Catholic school system.

Of course, the Catholic hierarchy and press must build up the parochial school system. It labels the public school as godless. It works as relentlessly as the "mills of the Gods" to secure public tax funds for parochial school support. It boasts of the constant growth of enrollment (now over four million). It vaunts its vast army of nun, priest and lay teachers. It is proud to claim a financial investment of billions of dollars.

An example of this exuberant self-evaluation is the following. Rt. Rev. Monsignor F. G. Hochwalt, Director, Department of Education, National Catholic Welfare Conference; Secretary General, National Catholic Educational Association, wrote in *Systems for Education,* January-February, 1955:

American Catholics strive continuously to make their schools educationally effective, philosophically sound, and religiously integrated. The measure of their success is found in the capable scholars and citizens who have come from this great educational system.

. . . At the top of the Catholic system stand the seminaries, major and minor, for the training of priests. In these institutions a very high level of scholarship maintains and the students may prepare themselves not only for parish and religious life, but for a life of deep learning and scholarship as well. The major seminary courses are built around the core of dogmatic and moral theology and scripture. Additional work in graduate philosophy, history, Church history, social sciences, languages, liturgy, speech and religious education round out carefully designed programs that serve the scholar and the parish priest.

The Jesuit priest, Robert C. Hartnett, is equally as positive in his praise of the parochial school and his further demand that it be supported by public tax funds:

My main argument, however, is this: Our Catholic schools are fulfilling a civic function, and the circumstance of their also fulfilling a religious function is no solid reason for penalizing American citizens who are exercising their constitutional right to have their children educated in religion in conjunction with their education in secular subjects.

No one has been bold enough to try to prove that parochial schools fail to teach children secular subjects just as well as do public schools. Do children in parochial schools learn less American history? Do they fail to learn arithmetic, spelling, English composition, geography, civics just as well as children in public schools? In competitions they frequently gain victories over public school children. The graduates of parochial schools are at least as prompt as any others in enlisting in the armed services of their country in time of war. If there is any score on which Catholic school children fail to measure up to public school children, we would like to know what precisely that score is.[1]

The Rev. John Paul Hagerty, Superintendent of Schools, Archdiocese of New York, said:

Catholic schools make good citizens. "Be a good Catholic," Commander Shea wrote his son Jackie, "and you can't help being a good American." The curriculum in the Catholic school is concerned with those subjects which prepare for the life here and now as well as for the one hereafter. Emphasis on good citizenship is stressed.

The children in the Catholic elementary and high schools follow a course of study that is basic, fundamental, sound. The texts in use are standard. Each diocese is free, however, to suggest changes, to effect emendations, to produce their own resource manuals. But by and large what differences there are, are very minor. The association of diocesan superintendents in national and regional groups promotes this uniformity of approach and the pooling of resources in matters curricular is frequent.

The Church is engaged in education for one purpose only.

Its primary objective is to bring men to a knowledge and love and service of God. What the Catholic school contributes over and above to the complete and rounded growth of the individual is subsidiary to its fundamental concern to assure the eternal salvation of all of its children.[2]

The vast parochial school system is so obviously a separatist system and so productive of division in the youth of America that the hierarchy must constantly protest to the contrary. In his Encyclical on Education, Pope Pius XI said:

They do not intend to separate their children either from the body of the nation or its spirit, but to educate them in a perfect manner most conducive to the prosperity of the nation. Indeed a good Catholic, precisely because of his Catholic principles, makes the better citizen attached to his country and loyally submissive to constituted civil authority in every legitimate form of government. . . .

Membership in the Church does not require that the Catholic isolate himself from those of his neighbors whose persuasions in matters religious differ from his own . . . Outside the Church there are multitudes of men and women who are people of good will whose lives give evidence of the noble ideals they cherish and who are intensely devoted to everything that promises a fuller measure of human happiness.

The *Catholic School Guide* published by the Catholic NEWS of New York asks:

1. *Why does the Catholic Church have her own schools?*

To teach youths how to "think, judge and act constantly and

consistently in accord with right reason illumined by the super-natural light of the example and teaching of Christ.

"For precisely this reason, Christian education takes in the whole aggregate of human life, physical and spiritual, intellectual and moral, individual, domestic and social, not with a view of reducing it in any way, but in order to elevate, regulate and perfect it, in accordance with the example and teaching of Christ."—Encyclical on Education, Pope Pius XI.

In the first place, Catholic parochial schools exist not because of the desire of Catholic parents or children for religious schools but because of the edicts of Canon Law, the encyclicals of the Popes, and decision of the American Catholic hierarchy.

In 1884, the American Catholic hierarchy, assembled in the Third Council of Baltimore, decreed:

Near each church, where it does not yet exist, a parochial school is to be erected within two years from the promulgation of this Council and is to be maintained in perpetuity, unless the bishop, on account of grave difficulties, judge that a postponement be allowed.

A priest who by his grave negligence prevents the erection of a school within this time, or its maintenance, or who, after repeated-admonitions of the bishop, does not attend to the matter deserves removal from that school.[3]

The head of every parochial school is, therefore, the pastor of the adjacent sponsoring Church. Pastors are appointed by the local bishop. They are not elected or "called" by the local congregation. They are appointed by the bishop, not because of their interest in education, or their ability as teachers or their pre-eminence in the arts and sciences. They are appointed because of their administrative skill, their success in raising money and their personal loyalty to the bishop and the hierarchy.

The encyclicals of the Popes and the public statements of American bishops (particularly when demanding tax funds for parochial schools) constantly emphasize the rights of parents in education. *In the parochial school, parents have no rights.* They have no voice in the location, the size or cost of the school building. They cannot vote for a school trustee (there are none), decide on a principal, or have a voice regarding the education or personality of a teacher. They have nothing to say regarding textbooks or curriculum.

The Parent-Teacher Association, when it exists in a parochial school, is a mannequin, preserved for window dressing and for raising money for parish activities. Most pastors do not even tolerate a P.T.A. It is risky for its officers to come in contact with those of the independent public P.T.A. groups at city and regional councils. Such contact might tempt them to meddlesome questioning of the conduct of the parochial school. In the whole state of Arizona in 1954, there was not a P.T.A. unit existing in any Catholic parochial school. Mothers' clubs were a more pliable substitute. In the 8,493 Catholic elementary schools in the United States in 1953, only one hundred and twenty-five had Parent-Teacher Associations, according to the National Congress of Parents and Teachers, December 17, 1954.

Roman Catholics do not have the right to choose between the parochial and the public school. They are forbidden by Canon Law from attending anything but a parochial school. "Catholic children shall not attend non-Catholic, indifferent that are mixed, that is to say, schools open to Catholics and non-Catholics alike." (Canon No. 1374)

In many American dioceses, where there are sufficient or nearly sufficient Catholic schools, the canon is enforced under penalty of mortal sin and the refusal of absolution as long as the children remain in a public school.

Some pastors have used this threat of sin as a club to force financial contributions from parents. A woman in Brooklyn wrote:

. . . In talking to Mary tonight I related to her a tale of the trouble I had in trying to get my child into parochial school about last May. He was considered ineligible because I had not paid a $150 pledge that I made to the Church. . . . This has been going on for some years, at least here in New York.

When I went to register my son, I had paid $1 and no more on a pledge of $150. The man that sold me the pledge told me in so many words that I would not even have a chance of getting the children enrolled if I did not make a pledge. I explained at the time that I was in no financial position to sign my name to such a statement. He assured me that if I at least promised to try it would be a chance. . . . (*The family lived in a public housing project.*—Author.)

When time came for enrollment I went to see the pastor with (isn't this awful) $5. He would not take my money, and he assured me that, since I had not paid anything, I could not be considered. He said that they could only consider those who paid in full, or at least half. I know a girl who paid for at least 4 or 6 months and was refused. . . .

In some churches, the pledges run much higher. These are usually made in order to pay for a new school, church, youth center, etc.

The nuns who teach in parochial schools, including the "nun principal," are also subject to the pastor in all matters of textbooks and curriculum.

With teaching nuns, too, loyalty comes before learning and a solid faith is much preferable to the inquiring mind. The attitude that must pervade the entire school system is expressed in the Constitution of the Franciscan Order:

269. No Lector shall be appointed who is not commended without reserve for his morals, faith and docility to the Holy See.

278. The Lectors and all the Friars (priests) are forbidden, in virtue of holy obedience, to dare publicly or privately to teach, defend or approve any erroneous or suspect doctrine or opinion savoring in any way of modernism, or contrary to sound morals.

CHAPTER THREE

The Three S's: Sex, Sin and Satan

The American public assumes that in the parochial school system Catholic students are taught the same basic moral code that prevails in the non-Catholic Judeo-Christian western world. They take for granted that the same values regarding integrity, property rights and personal sexual morality are taught to Catholic children as are taught in the non-Catholic American home.

In my experience, this is not true. The main differences are: (1) the use of a full time school system to "drill in" effectively the Roman Catholic concept of sin; (2) the idea that sins vary in offensiveness to God (mortal and venial sins); (3) the over-emphasis on sins of sex, with the added constant connotation that such things are "nasty" and "filthy" as well as sinful; (4) the comparative under-emphasis of the immorality of violations of property rights and verbal integrity (stealing and lying and civil law); (5) the use of the ceremony of confession throughout the school years to reinforce these teachings, particularly regarding sex, in the depths of a child's soul.

47

The non-Catholic child learns the basis of morals at home and in Sunday school. We were drilled in "morals" as well as "faith" all the five full school days of the week. The concept of sin was not taught only in the catechism class, where it was merely more intensely done, but also between classes, and interwoven through all manner of subjects so that the spirit of Pope Leo XIII may be fulfilled "not only at certain hours to teach Catholic religion to children but that all other subjects must also be made fragrant with the odor of piety."

To the "man-in-the-street" Catholic, the aspect of mortal sin that causes him to pause in fright (and frequently in later years, as a reaction of revolt, to reject the whole Catholic system as fantastically ridiculous) is not the offense against God involved in sin. It is the threat of hell.

To the Catholic child, even at the age of seven, eight or nine, hell is a vividly real thing. By that time already it had been depicted to me so often in word and picture that I could see and almost breathe its leaping, lunging flames. The exquisite tortures of Dante's Inferno are crude in comparison with what I was taught of the metaphysical refinements of hell as I progressed to the heights of Catholic education. There were voluminous expoundings of the theologians, the mystics and the "retreat masters" regarding the intensity of that fire, its ability to sear yet never destroy, and the "fact" that prior to the end of the world, when bodies shall be reassembled, that fire can burn also the soul, a pure spirit which has no material parts capable of combustion.

I learned to picture hell as an undulating sea of flame, burning the human souls within its depths, yet never consuming them, lapping as restlessly and as endlessly on

the shores of eternity as the rumbling surf of the Pacific
Ocean pounded the beach near our seminary in Santa
Barbara.

As frightening to me as the intensity of hell fire in the
punishment of mortal sin, was the unendingness of that
fire. Many similes were used to try to convey the extent
of eternity to minds accustomed only to the limitations of
time.

One comparison has become a classic in the Roman
Catholic world. It is mentioned in *Under Orders* by the
ex-priest of the Paulist Order, William Sullivan, who became a Unitarian minister. It goes like this: If God were
to send a bird once every thousand years to peck and take
away one grain of the earth's substance, it would take un-
counted billions of years to destroy this planet. Yet, when
this would have been accomplished, the eternal tortures
of the damned in hell would be only beginning.

This picture of mortal sin, of its consequences and the
duration of these consequences, was taught to me and is
taught to every Catholic child in every parochial school
in America.

A venial sin is an omission of a duty or a violation that
only slightly arouses the wrath of the Almighty. The Baltimore Catechism defines it: "Venial sin is a less serious
offense against the law of God, which does not deprive the
soul of sanctifying grace and which can be pardoned even
without sacramental confession." Rev. J. Noldin defines
it thus: "Objectively venial sin is an action which violates
the moral order and divine law only slightly, or it is an
action which does not seriously disturb the moral good,
towards the preservation of which the moral order is
established by divine law."

An accumulation of venial sins cannot add up to a mortal sin, because they are different in nature. However, the catechisms and theology textbooks stress the obvious fact that facility and familiarity with venial sin can make mortal sin easier to commit.

Hell fire is not punishment for venial sin. God makes man atone for these lesser violations by the vicissitudes of this life and by confinement to the fires of purgatory if one should die without pardon.

Forgiveness for venial sins is very easy to obtain. They may be mentioned in the confessional, but they need not be. They may also be wiped off the soul by a prayer called "the act of perfect contrition." As little children, we learned this by rote together with the "Our Father" and "Hail Mary." Both children and adults are urged to recite this prayer every night lest the Lord take them in their sleep and they be plunged into purgatory.

In fairness it must be pointed out that, in spite of the vast distinction between mortal and venial sin, the Catholic Church uses strong emotional means to dissuade members from venial sin. "Venial sin is a great evil—next to mortal sin it is the greatest evil in the world, worse than the most painful sickness or the most dreadful form of death."[1]

In parish "missions" (the equivalent of Protestant "revivals"), and "retreats" (days of concentrated prayer and preaching), venial sin was pictured to us as worse than the greatest cataclysms of nature, as more evil than any destructive plague, as more horrible than the combined destructiveness of all the world's atom and hydrogen bombs. But this eloquence did not for long affect us. Our moral reflexes had been so conditioned that a sin was not serious at all if we did not have to confess it and if we could not be sent to hell for having committed it. Our norm of right or wrong was quite selfish. Our lode star was hell—the welfare of our fellowman rarely concerned us.

In the classroom and in the confessional the greatest moral emphasis that I can recall was on sex. It began the day I stepped into St. Francis School.

Catholic theology teaches that every violation of its sex standard, no matter how insignificant, will send the soul to hell. "All directly voluntary sexual pleasure is mortally sinful outside of matrimony. This is true even if the pleasure be ever so brief and insignificant. Here there is no lightness of matter."[2]

It is important to remember that in these "voluntary sensual pleasures," which are mortal sins, should be included looks, touches, kisses, jokes, songs and even thoughts.

The Roman Catholic catechism taught us that the deliberate mental intention or desire to commit any sin is as bad as the act itself. However, only in matters of sex, is the mere thought a sin, much less a mortal deadly sin. It is a sin to plot and desire a murder. It is not a sin to think about murder. But in matters of sex, it is a mortal sin not only to "covet" one's neighbor's wife but also to merely abstractly *think* about the slightest thing remotely connected with sex—the pleasure of a genuine kiss, or the satisfying beauty of a woman's body.

All of this is taught in parochial schools to little children years before adolescence and the onset of puberty. They are sore put to know what the good nuns and priests are talking about.

Another thing that confused us as parochial school children is the imputed "nastiness" of things sexual. All Catholic catechisms and moral theology textbooks refer to violations of the Church's sex code (presumed to be God's code) as "impurity." This word is not used for any other type of sin. The connotation is developed in the child's mind of something physically dirty, or filthy or nasty, or foul or decayed. Fr. Kirsh calls sexual thoughts "rotten." Fr. Jone in *Moral Theology* constantly refers to the genital organs as "indecent" parts of the body. The whole pattern of Catholic morals ties the sex urge to the concept of degradation, the idea of "fallen" man. Pope Pius XI in his encyclical on the Christian Education of Youth calls sex "this infernal hydra" destroying "with its poison so large a portion of the world."

In spite of the constant emphasis on the sinfulness of sex, we were not instructed in what sex is. We frequently thought that adultery meant relieving nature at improper times and places. We thought that "impure" thoughts referred to thinking of our own bodies.

To me, Roman Catholic parochial school sex instruction was a negative thing, over-emphasizing in a confusing way the sinfulness and nastiness of sexual thoughts, words and actions, while telling me nothing of the purpose of these functions which all the prohibitions have spotlighted.

The angels and devils were pictured as battling for my adolescent soul.

Some of my friends doubt me when I tell them that we were warned that it could be sinful to bathe under a needle spray shower because the tingling effect might cause erotic reactions and tempt us to the "solitary sin." Catholic theologians and nuns have moral nightmares about masturbation and rail so against it, particularly in the confessional, that they undoubtedly remind the youngsters of it.

At this point, it might be well to discuss the question, or problem, of homosexuality among the clergy or the nuns.

It is commonly assumed that this practice is very common among the celibates of both sexes in monasteries and convents. If it is, I was too stupid or innocent in my twenty-seven years in a seminary and the priesthood to recognize it.

After leaving the priesthood and learning the facts of life, I could look back and feel that the affection that the famous Mexican Archbishop Orosco y Jiminez had for me might have been suspect. He was at least seventy when exiled from Mexico by President Calles. I was (in my early twenties) a theology student at Santa Barbara Mission. I had become his chauffeur and personal valet when he stayed at our monastery. Whenever I came to serve him, he embraced me with a vigorous kiss that I later learned could be described only as a "soul kiss." At the time I was embarrassed, but acquiesced to what I thought was merely an old Spanish custom.

"Thou shalt not steal" is the Seventh Commandment in the Douay (Roman Catholic) version of the Bible. A theological discussion of this commandment would presumably be confined to theft.

But the organization of the subject matter of moral theology is traditional and rather arbitrary. So the Seventh Commandment, in all theology textbooks, covers, besides the sinfulness of theft, morality of the following: ownership of property, marital property rights, contracts in general and property and building contracts in particular, agencies, partnerships, auctions, monopolies, brokerages, gambling, speculation, insurance (life and accident), last wills and testaments, inheritances, restitution and bankruptcy.

Noldin, in his *Summa Theologiae Moralis,* devotes two hundred and twenty-three pages to the Seventh Commandment; but only fifteen pages are concerned with the nature and sinfulness of stealing.

In St. Francis School, we were taught that stealing is wrong. But there was much confusion in our minds as to how wrong it was. It was not nearly so wrong as "bad" thoughts or "impure" actions because it was not talked about so much. Also those sexual things are mortal sins and the only stealing a child knows of is merely a venial sin. It is so small a sin that he doesn't even have to confess it.

I can still remember stopping as a boy in the early morning hours in Sacramento while delivering the San Francisco EXAMINER, and stealing milk and doughnuts from the stoop of a little corner store. I felt no effective guilt because it was only a venial sin. But a passing "bad" thought sent me scurrying to confession.

The catechism says: "A sin of theft is either mortal or venial, depending on the circumstances, especially on the amount stolen and on the financial condition of the person from whom it was stolen."[3]

We were confused by the doctrine that there is a difference in the seriousness of the sin if the theft be from an ordinary individual or a rich person or organization. If from an individual, any amount less than a full day's wage is only a venial sin. If from a wealthy victim or the state, a bank, a hotel or other institution, we could steal up to forty dollars without committing a mortal sin—no hellfire and no confession necessary. The modern textbooks, because of the devaluation of the dollar, have raised this amount to one hundred dollars.[4]

All of this confusion about property rights is taught by the theologians who train the priests who train the nuns who train the four million children who are in the parochial school system.

In the moral culture of America, truth, both verbal and written, has always been important. It has been the basis for the dealings between man and his fellow. Our pioneers boasted that a "mans' word was his bond" and agreements involving vast sums of money or the safety of lives were sealed with only the clasp of a hand.

With the complexity of a growing nation, agreements had to be reduced to written contracts; and before the courts of the land the truth of a man's word was confirmed with an oath.

Truth and integrity are as vital to the continuance of our democracy as "sacred honor" was to its beginning.

It should be shocking to Americans to know that Catholic children in parochial schools are not taught that truth is of paramount importance. We were taught that the violation of truth—the lie—is of itself merely a venial sin which need not be confessed.

"A lie as such is not a grievous (mortal) sin, for it is not a serious inordination against nature, nor a grave abuse or misuse of a faculty; it cannot be likened to suicide, murder, contraception, each of which completely subverts the order of nature and tends to the extinction of the race."[5]

Lying becomes a mortal sin only if some other virtue

besides veracity, such as charity or justice, is gravely violated.

The catechism and Roman Catholic theologians go a step further. It was shocking at first for me and my fellow students to accept the teaching that some forms of deceit, which all Protestants would brand as lies, are not sins at all. These are called "mental restrictions"—the deliberate withholding of truth even when done for the purpose of confusing or misleading another.

A "strict" mental restriction, i. e., when words used are so phrased that even the shrewdest person can't decipher them and discern the truth, is a lie.

But a "broad" mental restriction is one where the truth is there or implied, if the listener is alert enough to catch it. Examples are: "The lady is not home"—meaning "to you;" "I do not know," i. e., "anything I want to tell you;" "I don't have the ten dollars"—meaning "to lend to you." These circumventions are not only taught not to be lies but for sufficient reason (to be determined by the individual) they may even by fortified with an oath.[6]

The textbooks go so far as to state that the oath of office taken by the President, Congressman, Governor, Judge, etc., if the person be a Catholic, must be taken with the mental restriction that his upholding of the Constitution and laws is subject to their non-conflict with the laws of the Catholic Church.

In lecturing across the country, I have found non-Catholics extremely interested in the ceremony of confession. They want to know if Catholics really tell all, if they really believe that a man, the priest, can forgive sins and if the man, the priest, sincerely believes that he has the power to forgive them.

It never occurs to them, however, nor to most Catholics, to think of this ceremony as not merely a soul washing ritual but as an adjunct to the parochial school system. It is so much a part of that system that the confessional might well be called another classroom—the private class room for individual instruction.

CHAPTER FOUR

The Mystique

Extremely important in the Catholic school system's preparation of its children—particularly of its chosen elite, its "shock troopers"—is its emotional indoctrination.

Even the most air-tight logical reasoning from the Bible or history could not alone keep Catholic children in its school system and make them so loyal that they will freely dedicate their lives as priests or nuns. It could not convince laymen to live the Church's laws to the letter in their own lives and to sacrifice until it really hurts to support the Church and actively take part in its varied programs. The good "shock troopers" are dedicated. Dedication is not a rational but an emotional thing.

Peter the Hermit didn't lure the vast Children's Army of the early Crusades to their death through reason. None of the Crusades was based on reason. The frenzy to conquer the Holy Land and recover the Holy Grail was nothing but emotion.

In our own time, we have witnessed the skillful use of emotion by Hitler. Martial music, gigantic stadium rallies and parades of goose-stepping storm troopers drew the German people behind him and to destruction better than millions of words could ever do. Mussolini did the same.

The Roman Catholic Church has been the master of playing on human heart strings for many, many centuries. The Crusades were but one example. The miracle is another. The development of liturgical music, the splendor of the medieval cathedrals and even the horrors and murders of the Holy Inquisition were designed to sway the faithful by their emotion—not their reasoning.

Integrally interwoven through the Catholic parochial system is the concomitant use of emotional means to train and control Catholic children, especially the "shock troopers." It was very effective insofar as I was concerned.

An understanding of this emotional "education" is extremely important. It is more effective and far more lasting in the lives of good Catholics than anything in the school curriculum. They may forget the spelling, arithmetic and geography. They will undoubtedly forget the Latin, the algebra and the geometry. But they will never forget the rosary, the Mass and, especially, the ever-present threat of the yawning fires of hell, should they defy not only the law of God but also the law of the Church.

This emotionalism began the day I entered St. Francis school.

It was intensified by the rituals and devotional practices of Catholicism, such as masses, novenas, congresses, missions and retreats.

The emotional sublimation of sexual and sensual love is the inspiration that carried me and thousands of Catholic boys and girls through seminaries and convents.

Little children are early acquainted with the "tokens"

of Catholicism. The nuns gave us religious images as inducements to study. These, at first, were usually "holy pictures" representing Jesus, Mary, Joseph, the Guardian Angel and saints, popular with individual orders or congregations of priests or nuns.

As rewards for effort, medals were frequently given. These represented the same sacred personages, but they could be worn on chains around the neck or on key rings. Statues came next, usually of Jesus or the Virgin Mary, varying in size from tiny pocket versions in leatherette pouches, to Kewpee doll heights, won as prizes at church bazaars and intended to adorn our dressers or home altars.

In spite of the protestations of the hierarchy, some Catholics consider statues and holy pictures almost as living beings. A married woman came to me to complain about her husband's infidelity when she was out of town. "I told him it would have been bad enough if he had met this woman in the park or in an automobile; but he took her into my own bedroom, right under the eyes of my own saints on the wall."

Immediately after our first communion, during the next week, we were "inducted" into the "Scapular of Our Lady of Mt. Carmel." The scapular is made of two pieces of cloth approximately one and one-half inches square attached by two cords fourteen to eighteen inches long. One pad of cloth bears the image of Jesus, the other that of Mary. The ensemble is intended to hang over the shoulders—the scapula.

The wearing of the scapular under one's outer garments conveys very rich indulgences—which meant nothing to us as little children.

The custom of wearing this scapular goes back seven hundred years to a Carmelite Monastery near London. There the Virgin Mother, surrounded by a host of jubilant angels, appeared to St. Simon Stock, handed him a model of the scapular and uttered these words: "Receive this Brown Scapular. It is a safeguard in danger, a pledge of salvation. Whosoever dies while wearing my Scapular will never see the eternal flames of hell."

If the cloth scapular becomes too inconvenient, such as showing embarrassingly through a girl's dress, the scapular medal may be substituted and carried in a pocket or the girl's purse. The same indulgences are gained.

Since the Carmelite Scapular has proved so popular and so profitable, other scapulars have been offered by various religious Orders. A popular one now is the green scapular, endowed with blessings as a result of a vision. Another type of the brown scapular carries the blessing of the Franciscan Order. The Roman ritual gives the approved blessings for fifteen different kinds of scapulars.

The most popular "charm" of the Roman Catholic world presented to us was the St. Christopher medal. It is a semi-ecclesiastical insurance of safe travel by land, sea or air. "Christopher" comes from two Greek words meaning "Christ-bearer." The saint was a legendary, simple-minded Paul Bunyan who wanted to serve God. A wise priest advised him to use his brawn carrying people across a shallow but swiftly flowing river. One day a child asked to be ferried across. The muscular ferryman hoisted the youngster over his shoulders and blithely strode into the stream. The child became heavier and heavier until the weight became unbearable. The man asked the boy what made him so heavy. "You are carrying the one who carries the world." It was the child Jesus.

On the usual St. Christopher medal, the child is poising a ball surmounted by a cross. The ball is the earth and the cross represents the final submission of humanity to the Catholic Church. We were led to the conclusion that, if Christ entrusted himself to St. Christopher, everyone else can.

St. Christopher medals, stamped in aluminum, can be purchased for a few cents. They range upward to those of sterling, gold or porcelain. They are made for money clips, for pocketbooks, for automobiles and air liners, or to hang around the neck. The true use of St. Christopher medals is found in the cards attached to the medals in the dime and variety stores, "A good luck charm for travelers."

We were encouraged to openly wear medals and crucifixes around our necks. This was to serve a three-fold purpose: the gaining of the indulgences attached to such devotion; the proud profession of the Roman Catholic faith; identification as a Catholic in case of serious accidents with the resultant assurance that a priest will be called to give the "last rites."

The wearing of such medallions seems to have increased among young men since the war. It may be a carry-over of the familiarity of chains around the neck with the attached "dog tags." I can never cease marvelling at the inconsistency of our hospital's Catholic doctors, nurses and orderlies wearing these medals, particularly of the "Virgin Mary," as they enter our operating rooms to assist at abortions, sterilizations and every surgical procedure condemned by their Church.

The "spiritual bouquet" is a religious phenomenon that is peculiarly Roman Catholic. It is an offering to God, for some one or some cause, of an accumulation of prayers and good works. These may be attendance at Mass, visits to a church to pray before the holy Host, the pious reception of holy communion or ejaculations. The latter, theologically, are short prayers.

The Arizona REGISTER informed its readers a few years ago, that the children of only thirteen parochial schools offered the bishop a spiritual bouquet to help with his million-dollar drive for a new seminary. The children offered 14,978 Masses, 10,250 communions, 28,670 visits, 115,917 special prayers and 1,561,370 ejaculations.

A famous Jesuit army chaplain of the first World War tried to recite one hundred thousand ejaculations every day to gain vast indulgences for the souls in purgatory. While in the seminary, I tried to emulate him by reciting "Jesus, Mary, Joseph" under my breath all day long. Each recitation credited one hundred days' indulgence to the poor souls.

Medals, pictures and prayers of this kind are called sacramentals. The word distinguishes them from the sacraments, such as confession, which are taught to have spiritual power of themselves because of their "institution by Christ." The sacramentals have an indirect spiritual effect, due to the spirit of the user and the blessing of the Church.

One of the most ancient of the sacramentals is the "blessing." There are blessings for almost every conceivable thing or function, from the blessing of a threshing machine or of holy water to the "churching" of women after childbirth.

The Roman Ritual (Rituale Romanum) contains two hundred pages of blessings. There are special blessings for libraries, printing presses, church organs, herbs, seeds, processional banners, private chapels, archives, cornerstones, fishing boats, railroads, wagons, airplanes, bridges, fountains, fire, wells, fire engines, seismographs, blast furnaces, pastures, vineyards, granaries, mills, sick adults, pilgrims, pregnant women, sick children, clothing in honor of the Virgin Mary, clothing for the sick, sick beds, medicine, bread and pastries, beer, wine, butter and cheese, lard, birds, bees, silkworms, fish, horses, sick animals, stables and barns, mountain climbing instruments, hospitals, telegraph plants, electric generators, exterminating equipment and a multitude of blessings for sacred vessels, vestments, scapulars and religious garbs.[1]

Parochial school children learn in the early grades to have a tremendous awe of relics. We were allowed on special Tuesday services to kiss a relic of St. Anthony enshrined behind a glass plate in a golden monstrance. We knelt at the altar railing as the priest passed it along for our kiss and enabled us to transmit our coughs, colds, and other ailments to each other. St. Anthony was an early member of the Franciscan Order. His existence is reasonably established. The wondrous deeds, attributed to him as a means of effective preaching such as preaching in two cities at the same time, making donkeys and other animals talk, are legendary. So are his relics.

Relics constitute a very special form of sacramentals and not only grant indulgence and the blessings of the

Church but convey the spirit of the sanctity of the saints and frequently are said to produce miraculous results, especially in incurable diseases. Relics are of first, second and third classes. First class relics are parts of the body of the saint. A whole arm, leg, head or heart would be a major (*insignis*), first-class relic. Parts of the saints' clothing or personal effects would be second-class relics. Things, such as cloth, paper, etc., touched to his body would be relics of the third class.

The emotional indoctrination of parochial school children is intensified as they are initiated into the official liturgy and rituals of the Roman Catholic forms of worship.

Erich Fromm in his *Psychoanalysis and Religion* contends that ritual is essential to man. It is a "symbolic expression of thoughts and feelings by action. The need for ritual is undeniable and vastly underestimated."[2]

He does not detail what thoughts and feelings need ritualistic expression. But it seems obvious that among most men there are rituals for expressing obedience, respect, love, reverence and worship of the deity. In the rituals of authority, we have the uniforms of the police and fire departments, the panoply of ritual of our armed services, both as to uniforms, salutes, awards, promotions, channels and rank. Cub Scouts and Boy Scouts must have their badges and even the intellectuals, who boast of mentally rising above the masses, succumb to the liturgy or tradition when they don their academic robes and mortar boards to take part in a graduation ceremony. Our surrender to the dictates of Emily Post and the observance of the social graces are nothing more than the performance of the rituals of human intercourse.

Fromm says, ". . . the need for common rituals is thoroughly appreciated by the leaders of authoritarian political systems." Fascist and Communist regimes have satisfied this need in their mass political rallies.

The world's oldest and greatest religious political system, the Roman Catholic hierarchy, has made the fullest possible use of man's emotional need for rituals. It has supplied them for all ages, all moods and all occasions.

The most important of these is the Mass. The Roman Church has, over the centuries, taken the simple farewell gathering of the "last supper" and, with a kaleidoscope of color, an oriental ornateness of sacred vessels, and an overwhelming richness of symbolism, built up a liturgical ritualism that overwhelms the senses, especially of the young.

A proud antiquity is given to the ceremony by the very thought that the present form of the Mass, with the offertory, the consecration and the communion, was stabilized by Pope Gregory the Great and that he, too, developed or approved the first liturgical music, The Gregorian Chant, about the year 600 A.D.

I, personally, a nobody, the son of poor Irish immigrants, a boy who had shelled beans, mowed lawns and shoveled manure at the California State Fair—I became identified, through the Mass, with Pope Gregory the Great, with Palestrina in *O Bone Jesu*—(O Good Jesus) and *Adoramus to Christe*—(We adore Thee, O Christ) and Cesar Franck and the musical great of all Christian history.

As a child, I was awed by the vestments of the priest, the actions of the altar boys and the wall—the altar rail —that separated us from them. The Mass was the most important happening on earth, on Sunday when I must attend and on week days when I wanted to attend. I was taught that, as the daily renewal of Jesus Christ's sacrifice on the cross, it was infinitely more important than the Crusades, the Magna Carta, the Declaration of Independence, the Civil War or the emergence of America as a great nation of the earth.

When I was at St. Francis school, the Mass was an emotional ceremonial ritual that was all-encompassing and all-satisfying. The theology of transubstantiation (the changing of bread into a living God) meant nothing to me. All I felt was that something big, but unseen, called God was on the altar and that I could somehow "get a grip" on God by receiving communion. I felt an intense childish pride, like a youngster boasting of a successful hometown player, that my Church alone had this Mass which followed the dawn around the earth. I could be part of it among the pagodas of China, the cathedrals of Italy and the jungles of Africa simply by looking at a time schedule and projecting myself into those distant lands on a mystic magic carpet. By a "mental intention" I became united with those Masses all over the globe.

As a little boy, I felt sorry for Baptists, Methodists, Buddhists, Mohammedans and the rest. They were only small groups in isolated parts of the world. They were merely separated weak individuals without much direct help from God, because they didn't have the Mass. They were all outside the Father's House and lucky if they could get a few crumbs from the table.

The parochial school child, especially in a large parish, thrills, even though confusedly, to the more elaborate forms of the Mass. The high Mass is sung by the priest instead of being merely recited. The solemn high Mass is sung by three priests and offers tremendous opportunity for additional emotional pageantry in incense, candles, lights, flowers, golden vessels and vestments, additional dozens of red- and white-robed altar boys and a world of ancient and modern triumphal music.

The emotional climax is reached at the communion of a solemn Mass when the faithful rise and stream toward the altar. Many are ecstatic as they kneel and put out their tongues to receive the host. They are not worthy to touch it but as they return to their pews with heads bowed and hands folded, it is obvious that they are moved, not by theological conviction, but by emotional identification with this vast, ancient, beautiful thing. It was not unusual for me, not only as a child but also in later years, to weep as I witnessed and took part in this ceremony.

The splendor exceeds the child's comprehension at a solemn pontifical Mass (when the bishop is present), or an ordination to the priesthood or the consecration of a bishop.

And Mother Church can jerk him quickly from the heights to the depths of emotions in presenting the Mass for the Dead. *"Requiem alternam dona eis Domine."*— (Eternal rest grant unto them, O Lord.) The mournful chant of this and the *"Dies irae."*—(The day of wrath.) are as somber as the black candlesticks guarding the casket of the deceased. Even the candles themselves are dark, made of unbleached wax.

Roman Catholicism varies its emotional pattern to fit the seasons of the year. As parochial school children, we were carried along through the liturgy in a reliving of the life of Christ.

The season of Advent starts shortly after the beginning of the school year. It is the prelude to Christmas and symbolizes the thousands of years that Jewry waited for the Messiah. Neither "Jewry" nor "Messiah" meant anything to us as Catholic children; but we could visualize the "baby Jesus." The nuns told the story of the Wise Men and their gifts to the little Jesus. So we, too, should lure Jesus back at Christmas by our gifts. We offered him good deeds, and special prayers and money to buy orphan babies in China.

At Christmas time there is the "crib" or the "crèche" in every church and every parochial classroom. It is a replica of the stable of Bethlehem, with statues of Mary and Joseph, the Babe and an assortment of angels and shepherds. We would light candles, prepare flowers and pray to Jesus in thanks that He was a Catholic and belonged exclusively to the Catholic Church. Protestants who celebrate Christmas were to be tolerated in their ignorance that Jesus belongs to them, too. After all, when Jesus grew up didn't he start only one church and wasn't that the Roman Catholic Church?

The childish emotional self-immolation is most intense during the season of Lent. Adults must fast on all week days (only one full meal a day) under penalty of mortal sin. Parochial school children were morally forced to go along in acts of self denial. We "gave up" something for Jesus. The nuns insisted that we sacrifice candy, ice cream, cake, movies and other forms of entertainment; because Jesus fasted and suffered for us.

We used to save up all candy and chewing gum given us and, in the full exuberance of the Easter joy of the risen Christ, eat it all—plus the chocolate eggs and hard boiled Easter eggs. The depths of restraint were very real, as were the heights of joy; but they were emotional —certainly not intellectual or theological.

In the later years of high school and the seminary, the emotionalism continued. In the final years of the senior seminary and the beginning years of the priesthood, fear became a most powerful force. But, in the earlier days, loyalty and love carried us to heights of willing self-denial and self-immolation.

About 1926 the Ku Klux Klan burned a fiery cross on a hill opposite our seminary. The priests reminded us of the early martyrs of the Church and the Franciscans in America who had died for the faith. All of us were willing that night to die for Christ.

It was customary at Christmas time in Santa Barbara for the seminarians to attend midnight Mass at the old Spanish Mission Church. It was always a thrilling occasion for us. The Mass was preceded by a Mexican ceremony in the church called "Los Pastores." This was a procession of the shepherds and the Wise Men, gaily gowned and singing beautiful Spanish folk songs as they looked for the Niño, the baby Jesus. The "Missa Solemnis" was always superbly sung by the choir of theologians. The whole congregation thrilled to Cesar Franck's "Panis Angelicus" and the power of "Noel."

We were lifted to an emotional pitch that carried us back to Bethlehem. We worshipped at the crib and went out into the night with all the reassurance that the Light of the World was truly born again.

On Christmas Eve of 1926, our last year in the Junior Seminary, four of us felt too tense to sleep after the midnight Mass. We secretly and disobediently slipped out of the seminary grounds and walked down the hill on Garden Street toward the business district of Santa Barbara and the ocean beyond it. We were twenty years old. We did not go looking for girls, or for drinks or for food. We merely wanted to walk toward that band of silver thrown by the moon across the ocean and to exult in the fact that we belonged to the Roman Catholic Church.

One of us was the son of a German fisherman, another the son of a struggling appliance peddler, a third, the son of a French laborer, and I, the son of Irish immigrants. But that night we were not German or Irish or French or American. We were Roman Catholics. To us belonged the history of the Franciscan missionaries who had walked where Anacapa and Santa Barbara Streets now lead to the ocean. To us belonged the church that they had built a century and a half before and in which we had just heard midnight Mass. We were identified in our own minds with the whole Spanish Empire that brought those missionaries to California—the armies, the conquistadores, the Spanish galleons and their "Catholic Majesties," Ferdinand and Isabella. That night we were the heirs of what we thought the greatest, the most enduring organization on earth—the Roman Catholic Church. We were swept in our emotional enthusiasm back through cathedrals, and monasteries and coliseums; back through twenty centuries of history to the night when the angels sang and God became man—for the Roman Catholic Church alone.

That night the four of us solemnly and mutually dedicated our lives to continue on in the service of the Church. All four persevered and were ordained as priests.

All four of us have since quit the Franciscan Order and the Roman Catholic priesthood.

The next year I served my "Novitiate" at the San Luis Rey Mission north of San Diego. This is a year devoted entirely to meditation, instruction in the "religious" life and rule of the Franciscan Order, and preparation for taking the vows of poverty, chastity and obedience.

We were as secluded from the twentieth century as though we had been in Tibet. There were long periods of silence even at meals. We heard readings from the lives of the saints, particularly Franciscan saints. Throughout the year, sermons and conferences impregnated our minds with the thought that we were the favored of the Lord.

The emotional intensity reached such a point that I can recall climbing out of my cell window onto the roof over the patio colonnade and kneeling for hours during the night with my arms outstretched in a self-offering of complete immolation to God, for whatever purpose He wished to use me.

This same year I was chosen to prepare the Christmas crib, or the Bethlehem scene. This was a privilege and, I felt, an honor. It was to be done in the Sacred Heart Chapel of the ancient church. I planned to create a miniature Bethlehem with the stable, houses, pastures with real grass growing, a river with flowing water and, through a rheostat controlled by the water, a changing cycle over Bethlehem of dawn, daylight, dusk and night. It was a labor of love and my gesture to the Christ child.

In hanging the "sky" with its electric stars, I had to cover the statue of Christ. It was life size. As I stood on

the altar, I felt an uncontrollable surge of love for Christ,
I threw my arms around the statue and tenderly kissed
it. I was twenty-one years old.

This emotionalism surely seems childish and probably
disgusting to Protestants. But it is very real with devout
Catholics and especially with students for the priesthood
and sisterhood. It is the source of the tremendous personal
lifetime sacrifices made by sincere priests and nuns in
their ministry, in churches, hospitals, schools and foreign
missions around the world.

The ex-priest, William Sullivan, who had been a Paulist
priest and after leaving Catholicism became a Unitarian
minister, expressed this emotional bond of Catholicism
in words of rare beauty:

To a Catholic, who yields his soul to saturation in his faith,
that conception of the Church is of a depth and power that is
next to impossible for a Protestant to understand. The Church
is his aristocracy and romantic love; his household, where he
mingles with the holiest of all the ages, children, like himself,
of a mother solicitous and majestic, nurse of saints, yet mind-
ful of her sinners, and keeping in her heart memories incom-
parable, as far back as the age of martyrs and the missions of
the Apostles. When she takes him to her embrace, he ceases
to be a casual atom of humanity; he becomes an heir of the
ages, a citizen in the commonwealth of God; his name thence-
forward is entered in the vastest brotherhood ever known on
earth, and written through his august mediation in the book
of life above. The Church has saved civilization and will
save him, for her mission is to save. She has destroyed error
and will preserve him from it, for her calling is to be militant
against the seductions which would ruin souls, darken Christ
and defy God. For the mind she has light, for the heart
tenderness, for the imagination magnificence, for the soul
sanctity, for death consolation and a ministration of an im-

mortality of beatitude. Where is any likeness to her to be found? Where any rival fit to stand beside her in his heart? Nowhere while time shall be. Attachment, therefore, loyal and proud sonship and obedience perfect altogether, and perfect, most of all, when it is costly to be obedient, are his debt to her—the first, the last, the heaviest of all his debts.

It is a tremendous thing, this institutional idea and ideal; deeper and of greater power to elicit loyalty than was known even in Israel—the appointed monopolists of Jehovah's favor. It is at once beautiful and terrible; beautiful, pedagogically, as providing the individual with a world, giving to him who has no history a sense of history, and to him who is nameless an adoption into a family of the illustrious; and terrible, morally, because endangering personality by the prestige of overwhelming authority, and annihilating that solitude in which, by preference, the still small voice is mightier than earthquake and rushing wind makes itself heard for the guidance of aspiring man.[3]

The most all-pervasive, constant and certainly the most humanly appealing emotional "subject" of Catholicism's unique school system is the cult of the Virgin Mary—Our Blessed Mother—the Immaculate Conception and almost countless other titles under which she is venerated.

Mary is a far more important subject, although not formally, than any of the mundane items of the curriculum. It was so in the school I attended. It is so in every other Catholic school in America.

In the early grades, children are dressed in white and dedicated to Mary on the first of May. Special prayers are recited daily to her in the classrooms during "her month." We were taught the rosary with our alphabet. We were enrolled in Mary's scapular the day after our first communion.

The cult of Mary is not confined to the ignorant, backward nations of Catholicism. It is universal. It increases in tempo and manifestation as the child progresses through school. In moral classes on purity she is portrayed as the greatest example of purity, as the model of patience in poverty, as a supreme self-sacrifice of obedience in her willingness to be the mother of Christ.

Of the six "holidays of obligation" (on which Catholics must attend Mass as on Sunday) two are dedicated to Mary (three to Christ). Her statue or picture is as frequent in the classrooms as the crucifix. Feast days dedicated to her, her life, her activities, her joys and particularly her sorrows are scattered throughout the year.

Almost every city in America has at least one church dedicated to one of her titles. The bishops have consecrated the entire United States to her as the "immaculate conception," and they have built a national shrine in Washington under the same name costing millions of the faithful's money.

American bishops make it a well advertised point to visit the shrines of Lourdes in France and Fatima in Portugal on their way to see the Pope. The people who can't get abroad are encouraged to fasten little statues of Mary on the dashboards of their cars so they won't forget her as they drive.

As the Catholic school pupil progresses through a seminary, he finds a whole division in dogmatic theology *"De Mariologia"* (On Mariology). It comprises the traditions (sometimes allegedly backed by wrenched scripture texts) and the defined or declared dogmas of the Church on Mary. The culmination of it all is the teaching that Mary is the "mediatrix of all grace"—that Christ is the mediator between man and God only when that saving grace passes through the hands of Mary.

All this I was taught in the classroom of Catholic schools and from the pulpits of Catholic churches; and all of this I believed. The "Blessed Mother" added perhaps the feminine allurement needed to cement my loyalty to the Church. It helped make this organization not an abstract framework of history, doctrine and decrees but an enticing, embracing vision of flesh and blood.

I was certainly not the only Catholic child whose intensity of loyalty was fanned by the emotional appeal of Catholicism, especially the love of Mary. The following are a few examples of others. The first indicates also why many people still think Catholics worship statues.

From *Convent Glimpses,* a bulletin published by the Convent of the Sorrowful Mother in Milwaukee:

My dearest heavenly Mother:

Dear Mother, I met you for the first time in my parish church. You were so tall, dressed in loose and waving garments of attractive colors.

As I walked towards your altar, you looked so kindly at me. Your face was beautiful, sympathetic, and it inspired me with trust and confidence toward you. There were some tears on your cheeks and I asked you why you were weeping; you did not answer, but you looked so graciously toward me. You filled my soul with interior joy and happiness when I returned after confession to your shrine, where I thanked God for having forgiven me all my sins.

During my preparations for the happiest day of my life, for my first holy Communion, you, dear Mother of Sorrows, guided me and directed me in preparing a worthy dwelling for the reception of your Divine Son into my heart. On that beautiful day you whispered for the first time to me that you wanted me to dedicate and consecrate my life to the service of your Divine Son. Thanks, dear Mother, for all these graces. . . . Thanks, dear Mother, please, let me live and die as a worthy daughter of you, dear Sorrowful Mother.

Gratefully, your daughter,

Mary.

Evening climax . . . in the Crowning Glory Octave. After Benediction . . . lights out, Our Lady's statue borne on stalwart shoulders of our boys in blue . . . lighted candles, verses of the Lourdes Hymn and at the chorus, "Ave, Ave, Ave Maria," processioning clergy stopped and, together with the people, lifted candles on high. Tense expression, fear dimmed eyes, voices filled with feeling really saluted, hailed Mary, honored and crowned the loveliest lady of all time. From above front steps and out into the street and from beneath this fiery pageant . . . thousands of vibrant voices singing straight from the heart, repeatedly telling Our Lady she was their Queen and first love. "Growing days" . . . indeed!

Some students say the promotion of Mary is the hierarchy's realization of the extent of the "momism" and "mother worship" of our age, the emotionalism of Mother's Day, and shows the Vatican's shrewdness in exploiting the human instincts. Here is an example from *Novena Notes* (September 10, 1954), the pamphlet sent out by the Servite Fathers from the National Shrine of the Sorrowful Mother in Chicago:

Mary . . . an angel's salutation . . . the name that rises spontaneously to human lips in times of agony and stress. Mary

. . . virgins consecrate themselves in her name . . . youth in temptation calls upon it . . . old people bless . . . mothers and fathers pray it over sleeping baby forms and all love the name and bearer . . . the sweetest, the holiest, the purest woman who ever lived. Mary . . . it fits in extremes . . . hard bruising football at Notre Dame . . . centuries of toil and labor in a Cathedral monument of France . . . never ending beauty in the soft strains of an Ave Maria.

The sick stare dry-eyed into darkness . . . temptation to despair in the agony of loneliness. A rosary beneath the warm pillow gently each bead fingered and calm benediction and sweet peace in the prayer: "Holy Mary, Mother of God." Emptiness, loneliness and suffering become easier to bear and nights are less long. From the lonely sick to a hundred thousand people gathered in some vast stadium . . . the name Mary rises from American lips in petition and thanks. Yes, "Mary is a grand old name."

Catholics go to Mary with every problem that a child would cry about on his physical mother's knee. This intimacy is shown in the letters of thanks to the Virgin as acknowledged by correspondence to the *Novena Notes*. In the issues of September 3, 10, 17, of 1954, the following are some of the favors for which devotees of Mary wrote letters of thanks: "Home sold; soldier spared; husband recovers; daughter recovered; passed exams; senses restored; infection healed; foot saved; health restored; steady work; apartment found; better health; government job; survived surgery; safe delivery; business sold; healthy child; operation averted; troubles settled; X-ray O.K.; promotion; brother safe; suitable flat; son working; peace of soul; nerve cure; dental aid; niece returns; everything fixed."

When I was a boy, the devotion to Mary was a joyous

thing. The statues of Mary in our classrooms usually showed her with a halo of stars and her heel firmly implanted on the serpent's neck. We placed bouquets and red and green candles at her feet. May was Mary's month and we carried her statue surrounded and adorned with flowers around the school yard and through the church in a gay mood. We tossed all our petty problems to her along with the rose petals; and we expected her, like our own mothers, after hearing our stories, to hand us the cookie jar.

In the last few years, in spite of the dogma of the assumption of her body into heaven and the glory of the Marian Year, devotion to Mary has become overcast with sadness. It seems as though Catholics are despairing and are trying to drag Mary down to their level of gloom. Facts show that the masses of Catholics don't get along very well in this world. They are in the lower and lower-middle class mentally and educationally and sociologically. They work for a living. They don't create. Their lives are humdrum, routine and monotonous—born in pain and endured in misery, and misery loves company. So the sorrows of Mary throw something of a divine cloak or value over their own.

This is the only explanation I can think of for the intense emotional popularity of the *Sorrowful* Mother Novena. Unlike many other emotional fads in Catholicism, it has continued for years. The faithful are not obliged to attend these services, but they flock to them by the thousands. ("Novena" means "nine." A Novena means nine days, or weeks, or months of prayer or observance. A perpetual Novena goes on and on, nullifying the concept of the "Novena.")

Scattered throughout the *Novena Notes* are these phrases of a litany of sorrow:

> Mother most sad, pray for us.
> Fountain of tears, pray for us.
> Mother desolate, pray for us.
> Comfort of the wretched, pray for us.
> Mother bereft of thy child, pray for us.
>
> Harbor of the wrecked, pray for us.
> Terror of the treacherous, pray for us.
> Mother crucified, pray for us.
> Mother transfixed with the sword,
> Mother filled with anguish, pray for us.
> Mass of suffering, pray for us.

The saddest part of all this emphasis on sorrow is the unchecked financial exploitation of misery. The worship of Mary is one of the largest sources of revenue to parish churches and religious orders. Shrines and grottos dot the country and the world. At all of them, prayers are answered and donations before and after the favors are solicited. Offerings are made for medals, pictures, rosaries, statues, candles and votive lights. The faithful throughout the United States were solicited to contribute money and precious jewels for a diadem to be placed above a painting of Mary in Rome when the Pope proclaimed her Queen of the Universe in 1954.

The crudest form of fleecing ignorant Catholics is in the selling of "Lourdes Water." This water is from the "miraculous" spring at the Shrine of Our Lady of Lourdes in France. Advertisements in Catholic papers state that the water is not for sale. The required "offerings" are merely "shipping and handling charges." The procedure is reminiscent of the "donations" required in many Catholic churches for participation in bingo games, when courts have ruled that admission charges are illegal. The magazine *Mary Immaculate*, advertising Our Lady of Lourdes Grotto in San Antonio, Texas, proclaims "Genuine Lourdes Water Mixed with Grotto Sanctuary Water, sent upon request."

When thoughtful Catholics protest the exploitation and rackets attendant upon the worship of Mary, the hierarchy usually blames uncontrolled maverick shrines in various parts of the country. But the prelates endorsing and actually preaching at the Sorrowful Mother ceremonies in Chicago constitute the blue blood of the American hierarchy.

The Roman Catholic Church in America in the second half of the twentieth century is so dependent upon women that it would collapse without their self-immolation. The entire hospital system and parochial system could not exist without the nursing and teaching nuns. Not only must their sex be exalted but they must feel that they have an advocate in court—in heaven. It is smart to let the hereafter have its distaff side.

My experience has been that priests and bishops have a healthy respect for both teaching and hospital nuns and try to stay completely out of their internal convent affairs, including their politics. The struggles for power within convents are vicious and reminiscent of the legends of the Amazons and the stories of matriarchies. This world of women must have representation above.

Nuns teach their members that Mary is their trusted advocate. The following is from *Convent Glimpses*:

The Sisters *venerate* Mary as their Mother and patroness. From the first moment they awake until they retire, the Sisters are united with their heavenly Mother by frequent prayers and ejaculations. The short prayers prescribed for them when putting on their religious garments, express their love and fidelity to Mary. In spirit they received the veil from her as a pledge of a holy and spotless life, and when putting on the medal of the Sorrowful Mother, they ask her to place her image as a seal upon their heart. At morning prayer the Sisters consecrate to Mary their eyes, ears, mouth, heart, and whole body. During the visit to the Blessed Sacrament, they renew their consecration to Mary. Standing in spirit with Mary beneath the Cross the Sisters recite daily the Stabat Mater. Finally, in the evening prayer the Sisters implore her blessing and protection for the night.

I believe that the cult of Mary is probably the strongest tie holding people to the Catholic Church throughout the world. In my work in South Phoenix, for years I have observed people, especially Latins, who would violate every norm of ethics and morality, including those of the Catholic Church. Yet they would never be without a medal of Mary around their necks. I have known those who hadn't been to Mass or communion in years; but faithfully maintained their home altar to the statue of the "Virgin."

Among foreign shrines the best known to American Catholics are those at Lourdes and Portugal. Most Americans, especially tourists, are vaguely familiar with the one at Guadalupe in Mexico, near Mexico City, where Mary "appeared" to an illiterate youth, Juan Diego, in 1531. The Catholic *history* textbook, *How Our Nation Began,* digresses from the story of the United States to devote two full pages to this phenomenon. Mary's business on the occasion was to tell Juan Diego to hurry and tell the local bishop, a Franciscan, that she wanted a church built and dedicated to her on that spot. The bishop was skeptical and Mary had to appear three times (always to the boy—not to the bishop) and work the "Miracle of the Roses" before the bishop called in the architects.

Our Lady of Guadalupe has her counterparts throughout Latin America. All these apparitions of Mary are officially approved. In Cuba it is Our Lady of Charity de Cobre; in Honduras, the Virgin of Suyapa; in Colombia, Our Lady of Chinquinquira; in Venezuela, Our Lady of Coromoto de los Cospes. Brazil has Nossa Senhora Aparacida; Ecuador, the Virgin del Quinche; and Bolivia, Our Lady of Copacabana. An Indian of Paraguay started the devotion of Our Lady of Caacupe and Our Lady of Lujan has become the patroness of Argentina, Uruguay and Paraguay.

The "Grail" Press (Benedictine) offers color books for children of Our Lady of Guadalupe, Our Lady of Lourdes, Our Lady of La Salette, Our Lady of Pontmain, Our Lady of Pollevoisin, Our Lady of Knock, Our Lady of Fatima, Our Lady of Beauraing, Our Lady of Banneux, and Our Lady of the Medal. To these can be added Our Lady of Einsiedein, Our Lady of the Snows, Our Lady of Perpetual Help and many more.

In 1945 Pope Pius XII called Our Lady of Guadalupe the "Empress of America."[4]

American Catholics are now trying to get into the act. Mary has been chosen as Our Lady of the Airways, Our Lady of the Runways and Our Lady of Television.

A German Catholic priest, Father John Pinsk, was condemned by the Vatican (Arizona REGISTER, July 22, 1955) and his pamphlet ordered withdrawn from circulation because he placed Mary "on the same level as other creatures." He had concluded that there is no scriptural basis for the glorification of Mary. The *Osservatore Romanum* says that nineteen centuries of Catholic tradition are more decisive than the Bible and quotes Pope Pius XII as saying that the man who tries "to explain the Blessed Virgin's great dignity and sublimity from the Sacred Scripture alone, or who thinks these Sacred Scriptures can be explained without taking Catholic 'Tradition' and sacred teaching authority into account, is very much mistaken."

On September 5, 1936, Cardinal Patrick Hayes of New York gave his imprimatur to this story:

"A Bernardine Sister was shown in spirit the vast desolation caused by the devil throughout the world, and at the same time she heard the Blessed Virgin telling her that it was true, hell had been let loose on earth; and that the time had come to pray to her as Queen of Angels and to ask of her the assistance of the Heavenly Legions to fight against these deadly foes of God and man."

Bishop Thomas E. Molloy of Brooklyn gave ecclesiastical approbation to this prayer:

"In the presence of all the heavenly court I choose thee this day for my Mother and Mistress. I deliver and consecrate to thee, as thy slave, my body and soul, my goods, both interior and exterior, and even the value of all my good actions, past, present and future; leaving to thee the entire and full right of disposing of me, and all that belongs to me, without exception, according to thy good pleasure, for the greater glory of God, in time and in eternity. Amen."

The recent Marian Year is proof enough that the cult, or—as Pope Pius XII said in his official prayer—the "worship," of Mary is endorsed by the hierarchy.

In that official prayer composed for the Marian Year 1954, Pius XII stated:

Queen of the Most Holy Rosary, Refuge of the human race, Victress in all God's battles, we humbly prostrate ourselves before thy throne, confident that we shall receive mercy, grace and bountiful assistance, and protection in the present calamity, not through our own inadequate merits, but solely through the great goodness of thy Maternal Heart . . .

Queen of Peace, pray for us and give to the world now at war the peace for which all peoples are longing, peace in the truth, justice and charity of Christ. Give peace to the warring nations and to the souls of men, that in the tranquility of order the Kingdom of God may prevail. . . .

Give peace to the peoples separated by error or by discord and especially to those who profess such singular devotion to thee and in whose homes an honored place was ever accorded thy venerated icon (today perhaps often kept hidden to await better days): bring them back to the one fold of Christ under the one true Shepherd.

Obtain peace and complete freedom for the Holy Church of God; stay the spreading flood of modern paganism; enkindle in the faithful love of purity, the practice of the Christian life, and an apostolic zeal, so that the servants of God may increase in merit and in number. . . .

CHAPTER FIVE

Propaganda in The Textbooks

Aside from the classes in religion, the curriculum in
Catholic schools imitates that of the public schools as
closely as their more limited finances will permit. It frequently does not include manual training or shop, home
economics, or other courses requiring a great deal of
space or very expensive equipment.

Catholic school leaders maintain that, in the subjects
they do teach, they use standard textbooks common to
both public and parochial schools. They sometimes do;
but in subjects such as reading, history or literature, they
usually require their own texts with hierarchical endorsement or modified public texts approved by the Church.

The following is from the 1957 catalog (p. 7) of Harcourt, Brace and Co., New York:

ADVENTURES IN LITERATURE—CARDINAL NEWMAN
EDITIONS List.

A literature program based on the Mercury Editions. The
Catholic editors, Sister Marie Theresa, S. C.; Brother Basilian

87

Richard, F. S. C.; Sister Anna Mercedes, S. C.; and the Rev. Leo F. Halpin, have helped make this program fit precisely all of the *special* requirements of the Catholic high schools.

When I was a youngster, the "Benziger" readers were standard in parochial schools. They were positively Roman Catholic in tone and content. Reading texts now in use are more subtle. The books *We Talk, Spell and Write,* the "Cathedral Basic Language Program" for the first, second and third grades, project Catholicism by pictures. Nuns are shown in classrooms (as though only nuns are in classrooms). Crucifixes are shown on walls. Statues of Mary are in corners. The saints appear in drawing suggestions. Items of Catholicity are used as pictorial explanations of individual words. The word "back," for instance, is illustrated by a drawing of the back of a priest at the altar saying Mass.

Among the very Catholic texts are the grammar grade histories, *Before Our Nation Began* and *How Our Nation Began,* both from New York's William H. Sadlier, Inc., and bearing the "Imprimatur" of Cardinal Spellman. They are part of the "Christian Social History Series." The brightly colored picture covers do a selling job for the Church. The former shows a parade of solemn Crusaders carrying the Cross to Islam. The latter pictures a saintly Jesuit in a canoe bringing the Cross to receptive American Indians. These histories were produced in 1953 and 1954 in collaboration with the Curriculum Committee of the New York State Council of Catholic School Superintendents and are presumably in wide use in Catholic schools.

Before Our Nation Began is a history of civilization up to the founding of the American republic. It passes over the pre-Christian world in a perfunctory manner and then launches into some two hundred pages of pro-Catholic Church history of Europe.

The children (sixth grade) are also presumed to believe that Catholicism is the badge of aristocracy. On page five of *Before Our Nation Began* is the following dialogue between father and son:

"You get your religion from your great-grandparents. They were both Catholics when they came to this country. Naturally, they raised their children to be Catholics. In this way, their religion was passed on to you. This is the greatest gift they could have given you—it is the gift of the true Faith."

"But how did our great-grandfather and great-grandmother happen to be Catholics?" asked Jim.

"I suppose they got their religion from their parents," his father answered. "On your great-grandfather's side, perhaps the Faith can be traced to Saint Boniface or one of the other missionaries who worked in Germany. On your great-grandmother's side, perhaps it can be traced all the way back to Saint Patrick who brought the Faith to Ireland."

The Roman Church is pictured as the mother of learning, culture, art, literature, exploration and science. The Crusades constitute a selfless beneficial holy war. Luther and all Protestant leaders are belittled. The child gathers the impression that the principal result of the Reformation was internecine war, with the bulk of the killing being done by the Protestants. There is no mention of St. Bartholomew's Eve or the Inquisition or the hierarchy's part in the burning of Joan of Arc.

This is presumably a history textbook, not a defense of Catholicism. Following are a few random quotes:

"Our Lord said, 'Thou art Peter and upon this rock I

will build my Church and the gates of hell shall not prevail against it.' With these words He made Peter the head of the Church."

"Luther was wrong in disagreeing with the teachings of the Church. The Holy Spirit is always with the Church. The Holy Spirit protects the Church from error. Luther substituted his own judgment for the authority given to the Church by our Lord Himself."

"The Lutheran religion was a new religion, a religion that had been started not by Jesus Christ, but by Martin Luther."

"Henry VIII instructed Parliament to make him head of the Church of England. He then told the Catholics of England that they should no longer obey the Pope, not even in spiritual matters. The King, of course, had no right to do this. Our Lord Himself had made the Pope head of the Church. No king has a right to take this power away from the Pope."

"Mary was a Catholic and she tried to bring England back to the Catholic Church. The nobles planned to revolt against Mary. The Queen heard of these plans. She had some of the nobles put to death. For this reason many Protestants called her 'Bloody Mary.' The Queen, however, was merely trying to protect herself, her country and her Church. Even today, people who try to overthrow the government are often put to death."

"The Council of Trent put new life into the Church. The Council caused a real reformation of the Church. We call this the Catholic Reformation."

"These French Canadians are devout Catholics. As with the Spanish and the Portuguese, the greatest gift which the French brought to America was the True Faith."

"Today about one American out of every five is a Catholic. We Catholics of the United States should pray that more and more of our fellow Americans will realize that the Catholic Church is the one true Church."

It is doubtful if the many Protestants who send their children to Catholic schools because the "discipline is better" are acquainted with the "history" they are learning.

The companion history book *How Our Nation Began* treats the colonization of the New World and the beginning of our republic from the same sympathetic Catholic viewpoint. Leif Ericson, the devout Catholic who brought the "one true Faith" to Greenland, is shown as the true discoverer of America. The Catholic nature of the exploration of the Spanish and French is constantly re-emphasized, together with their kindness and solicitude towards the Indians. The apparition of the Virgin of Guadalupe near Mexico City is told as a fact in great detail. The story of the persecution of Catholics by Protestants in England and the colonies is stressed and Charles Carroll of Carrollton is pictured as a generous soul who, in spite of his sufferings, because of his Catholic faith, rose above his persecution and became one of the signers of the Declaration of Independence.

The same pattern persists in two more advanced textbooks of this same "Christian Social History Series." They are *A New Nation* and *A Nation United,* also approved by Cardinal Spellman and the Curriculum Committee of the New York State Council of Catholic School Superintendents. The foreword of *A New Nation* states:

This textbook would be incomplete without mention of the inportant contribution of the Catholic Church to the culture and civilization of our country. In every important event and movement in America from discovery and exploration to the present day, the Church has been a strong influence in building a Christian democracy and in defending it in every crisis. The authors show how the Church's teachings concerning family life, labor relations, rural and industrial problems, national and international policies, and interracial understanding have contributed to the betterment of our American way of life.

On page ninety-two of *A Nation United*, a cartoon depicts the contrast between Karl Marx and Pope Leo XIII with this caption: "Social reform was urged by Karl Marx and Pope Leo XIII. Marx said that owners and workers were enemies and he wanted the workers to revolt. Pope Leo said that all men are brothers and that they should work together for the good of all."

Not only is Leo XIII designated as the "Pope of the Workingman," but the impression is left that he was the greatest if not the only real leader of the American working man. Much is written (p. 92) about Leo XIII's advocacy of the "family living wage." But there is no mention of the fact that, by AFL-CIO standards, a "family living wage" has not yet been reached in the wage scales of Catholic Hospitals or of lay teachers in Catholic schools; although more than sixty years have passed since Pope Leo's encyclical.

The advanced readers for the seventh and eighth grades of the "Cathedral Basic Readers" by Rev. John A. O'Brien (Scott, Foresman and Co., Chicago, 1946 and 1947) are *Paths and Pathfinders* and *Wonders and Workers*.

In the first book, interspersed with selections from Joaquin Miller, Longfellow, Nathaniel Hawthorne, Thackeray, Mark Twain and Washington Irving, are such stories as "Father Damien Meets a Leper," "Father De Smet Finds Sitting Bull," etc.

The same is true of *Wonders and Workers*. Charles Lamb, Sir Arthur Conan Doyle, Charles Dickens, James Russell Lowell, Hans Christian Andersen and Sir Walter Scott share the book with the clerical writers, Bernard Hubbard, S.J.; Sister Madelena; Cardinal Newman; Hilaire Belloc; James Keller, M.M.; and James A. Van Der Veldt, O.F.M.

To enrich the literary background of Catholic high school pupils, the excellent four volumes of Harcourt, Brace and Co. Mercury Edition (1954) of *Adventures* were chosen. The "Cardinal Newman" edition of these books comprises the *Adventures in Reading, Adventures in Appreciation, Adventures in English Literature,* and *Adventures in American Literature.*

The preface of the first volume (p. vii) plainly states the intent to infiltrate the volumes with Roman Catholic thought:

The Cardinal Newman Edition of *Adventures in Reading* is an anthology that is designed to meet the needs and interests of students in Catholic high schools.

Throughout the four books of the Cardinal Newman Edition, the editors have sought to include literature that is both Catholic and catholic. They have given these books the substance and the direction of a Catholic philosophy of literature. Using the Mercury Edition of the *Adventures in Literature series* as their base, they substituted many new elections. In the teaching aids—study questions, reading lists, introductions, vocabulary studies, footnotes and glossary—they have incorporated whatever they felt was necessary to satisfy the requirements of Catholic high schools.

As Catholic youngsters pass into Catholic high schools, the "standard texts" in history become so slanted towards the Church that it is easy to understand why these pupils develop a feeling that the better things in the American way of life come from the Catholic Church, and the fact that the vast bulk of the colonists who fought for American freedom were Protestants was purely accidental. One of the most aggressive and divisive high school textbooks is *American History for Catholic High Schools* by Meng & Gergely (Sadlier, Inc., N. Y., 1954). It bears the approving imprimatur of Francis Cardinal Spellman.

The Catholic child can hardly help "getting his back up" when he reads on page four in the introduction comments about the early Protestant colonists: "In addition to these external forces against them, the builders of the new nation had to fight their own weaknesses. Having fled persecution, some of them paradoxically turned persecutors themselves. With hysterical intolerance they burned witches, hated Catholics, and almost destroyed the liberty they set out to find. . . . Then there were the heroes who planted the seeds of the Faith and nourished in spite of all danger. Every Catholic boy or girl knows about St. Isaac Joques, the Jesuit martyr, La Salle and the Mississippi, the Carrolls of the Revolution, Barry of the Navy, Prince Gallitzin of the Alleghenies, and Tekakwitha, the 'Lily of the Mohawks.' "

This text continues to repeat the theme (p. 13) that

America's beginnings were Roman Catholic. Not only does it elaborate on the Catholicity of Spain, Portugal and France and exaggerate their part in western colonization but it tries to identify the principles and loyalties of the American colonists with Rome. "Such were the beginnings of the Catholic spirit in America. The Europe that discovered *and explored* America was Catholic with a heritage of over a thousand years."

Democracy's debt to Catholicism is expounded on page seventy-four:

Democracy had its roots in Christian principles. Although the Colonial spirit of political liberty was closely linked with the progress of Englishmen toward self-government, the whole idea of the rights and responsibilities of the individual in society is drawn from Christian ethics. Early Catholic thinkers like St. Augustine (354-430), St. Robert Bellarmine (1542-1621), and Francisco Suarez (1548-1617) emphasized the equality of men. At the same time they balanced this concept of equal rights with the importance of obedience to the properly constituted authority.

Both Cardinal Bellarmine and Father Suarez made clear that the right to rule comes to the ruler from God, but indirectly through the people who give their consent. In other words, the people have a right to choose their own form of government and their own political rulers.

Even our country's Declaration of Independence becomes a Roman Catholic document (p. 94):

The Declaration expressed Catholic social principles. The one Catholic signer of the Declaration of Independence, Charles Carroll, was probably very happy to put his name to the document, for it was completely in accord with the basic principles of Catholic teaching.

According to Catholic doctrine, the state exists for the good of the individual. The individual is endowed with certain natural rights, because he is a person who is made to God's image. Those rights a state cannot give him nor take away from him since he possesses them because of his nature.

If we examine the second paragraph of the Declaration of Independence, we find this sentence:

"We find these truths to be self-evident, that all men are created equal, that they are endowed by their creator with certain inalienable rights, that among these are life, liberty, and the pursuit of happiness."

The rights included here are the "natural rights" that, as Catholic doctrine points out, belong to an individual. The right to "life" comprises such particular natural rights as security from all kinds of physical assault. The right to liberty means freedom to move about, to worship, to write and speak, and to obtain an education. The pursuit of happiness includes the right to own property and to contract marriage. These are civic rights which our American system of government guarantees to all inhabitants of the United States. As they are also the rights necessary to attain a reasonably happy life and the end which God intended, they are called natural rights.

Thus, the political ideals upon which our government was founded are entirely in agreement with Catholic principles." ...

This is American history as it is being taught now to millions of American Roman Catholic children.

CHAPTER SIX

Censorship in The Textbooks

The curriculum and textbooks of the Catholic parochial schools of America should be scrutinized by all adult Americans, Catholic and non-Catholic alike. They should examine them not only for the positive propaganda which is woven through Catholic textbooks and classes, but also for the negative propaganda. By this, I mean the elimination from textbooks, particularly in history and in civics, of significant events and official policies. This censorship is so crippling educationally that, if it were realized, it would be absolutely unacceptable to American citizens —even reasoning Catholic American citizens.

Four specific examples of this concealment or "watering down" of Catholic history and policy are the following: (1) The Holy Roman Inquisition; (2) The Council of Trent; (3) The Council of the Vatican; and (4) the relationship between the *principles* of American democracy and the official *teachings* of the Roman Church. This is done in the textbooks and schools, including Roman

Catholic high schools and the higher schools, the universities and seminaries.

The Inquisition is an "incident" that Catholic history teachers would prefer to forget. It is commonly ignored in high school Catholic histories and explained away in more "advanced" texts or in question columns in Catholic papers and periodicals.

It is portrayed, when attention is forced upon it, as an institution established for the legal ferreting out of heretics and the preventing of the spread of false doctrines. It is conceded to have been a desperate measure but excused as being needed by desperate times. The Catholic child learns that some inquisitors became imprudent, and indulged in unnecessary physical torture; but only to preserve the truth of the Catholic doctrine.

The general impression is given in the parochial school that the Church has been unjustly blamed for the national excesses of the Spanish Inquisition. In Spain, it is said, cruelty was the only possible deterrent to national destruction by the Jews and the Moors; but, within the Church itself, "inquisitor" became an honorary title, and physical torture for heresy and apostacy became rare and mild.

There is no doubt that the Popes and the hierarchy felt that they had the right to physically force religious conformity and to punish and execute non-conformists. They taught this right and they exercised it for centuries.

About the turn of the first millenium after Christ, the scattered bishops were charged with the inquisition into heresy.

In 1185, Pope Lucius III rebuked the bishops for their laziness, ordered them to visit their parishes once a year to arrest all suspected of heresy and turn them over to the state for punishment. Papal legates were empowered to depose bishops who did not act vigorously in stamping out heresy.

In 1198, Pope Innocent III had written to the archbishop of Auch: "We give you a strict command that, by whatever means you can, you destroy all these heresies and repel from your diocese all who are polluted by them. . . . If necessary, you may cause the princes and the people to suppress them with the sword."

In 1215 Pope Innocent ordered all civil authorities, under penalty of excommunication and loss of their realms, "to exterminate from the lands subject to their obedience, all heretics who have been marked out by the Church for due punishment." [1]

The statement of Innocent points up the fact that the initiative for the physical torture of heretics rests with the Church and that the state was forced to act merely as the executioner.

The full force and power of the Papacy was thrown against all who differed with Catholicism, by the famous bull of Innocent IV, "Ad Extirpanda" ("In Order to Exterminate"), issued May 15, 1252, for the administration of the Inquisition in Italy. It is undoubtedly one of the most detailed authoritative decrees of confiscation, imprisonment, torture and murder ever conceived by man. And it was directed, not against killers, rapists, arsonists or thieves, but against those who dared to worship God according to the lights of their own consciences.

Among the many details of the bull were provisions that anyone finding a heretic could seize him and take possession of his goods. The state was bound to arrest all accused, hold them in prison and execute within fifteen days all judgments pronounced against them through the Church inquisitors. All fines and confiscations, if such be the punishment, were to be divided in three parts, one to the city, one to the informers, and one part to the local bishop and the inquisitors.

This detailed law was ordered inscribed on all local statute books under penalty of excommunication for the officials and interdict for the city. The latter meant the prohibition of Church functions such as baptisms, Mass, weddings, funerals, etc. Any ruler failing to enforce the law was considered suspect of heresy himself, dismissed from his position and became ineligible for any civil position in the future.

An interesting sidelight of the bull was the Vatican's assumption of complete jurisdiction over the civil authorities.

The bull was reissued by Alexander IV in 1259 and extended to all Christendom in 1265. As Lea said: "To human apprehension the papal Inquisition was well nigh ubiquitous, omniscient and omnipotent."[2]

The punishments for heresy were fines, confiscation and destruction of property, torture, imprisonment for years or for life, or burning at the stake. It is interesting to note that burning at the stake enabled the Inquisition to inflict the death penalty, while still observing the Church's principle, *Ecclesia abhorret a sanguine.* (The Church shrinks from blood.). When the heretic was burned, he did not shed blood. Torture on the rack was also an acceptable method of extracting confessions of heresy—and, later, of witchcraft, which was considered akin to heresy.

How many heretics received these varying punishments can hardly be known. But it is certainly not true to say that burnings at the stake, carried out by the authority of the Papal Inquisition, were very rare. Records are admittedly scarce, but we read of eighty heretics being burned in Strassburg in 1212.[3] In Toulouse, six hundred and thirty-seven heretics were burned in fifteen years.

In a *Sermo generalis* (a pronouncement of convictions and penalties), in Toulouse in 1310, twenty people were ordered to make pilgrimages, sixty-five were condemned to life imprisonment and eighteen to death.[4] How many thousands of sincere, dissenting Christians rotted in dungeons or were maimed on the rack we can only guess. Will Durant summarizes this with the words: "Compared with the persecutions of heresy in Europe from 1227 to 1492, the persecution of Christians by Romans in the first three centuries after Christ was a mild and humane procedure."[5]

When the average lay Catholic is confronted with the horrors of the Inquisition, he usually shrugs off the atrocities with a remark such as, "Those were rough days, but how about the Protestant witch burning in Salem?" It has never been emphasized to him that in witch burnings, too, the Papal Inquisition more than set the pace.

In Salem, apparently the witch-burning center of early Colonial America, twenty "witches" were executed. There was another executed in Charlestown in 1648, and one in Boston in 1655.[6] This was, of course, barbaric.

Catholic students in their parochial schools are not taught that, under the Papal Inquisition, thousands upon thousands of witches were burned in Europe. The inquisitors, throughout the fifteenth and sixteenth centuries, indulged in orgies of persecution and death that shamed even the earlier Inquisition. Witches were burned by scores and hundreds.

Lea recounts the details: "A bishop of Geneva is said to have burned five hundred within three months, a bishop of Bamburg six hundred, a bishop of Wurzburg nine hundred. Eight hundred were condemned, apparently in one body, by the Senate of Savoy. . . . The spring of 1586 was tardy in the Rhinelands and the cold was prolonged. This could only be the result of witchcraft, and the Archbishop of Treves burned at Pfalz one hundred and eighteen women and two men, from whom confessions had been extorted that their encantations had prolonged the winter. . . . Paramo boasts that in a century and a half from the beginning of the sect, in 1404, the Holy Office (the Inquisition), had burned at least thirty thousand witches who, if they had been left unpunished, would easily have brought the whole world to destruction."[7]

The instruments of all this torture and slaughter, over a period of four hundred years, were not professional hangmen. They were Roman Catholic priests, very many of them Franciscan priests. They were men, who like myself, had been ordained as "other Christs," followers of the forgiving Galilean, sworn to offer the sacrifice of the Mass and wash away the sins of man with the blood of the Lamb.

As a history textbook, St. Mary's High School in Phoenix, Arizona, has been using (1954), the accepted text *Christianity and Civilization,* by James A. Corbett and M. A. Fitzsimmons, Associate Professors of History, University of Notre Dame, and Rev. Anthony Ostheimer,

Ph.D., published by William Sadlier, New York, 1947. The Imprimatur is by Francis Cardinal Spellman. In this textbook of more than eight hundred pages on the history of Christian (Catholic) civilization, the Inquisition is not even mentioned, nor is it mentioned in other Catholic history books I have received.

The Rev. J. V. Sheridan conducts the Question Box of "The Tidings" of Los Angeles. In the issue of May 10, 1956, the following questions were asked:

Q. As a potential convert I am interested in some specific information (not mere generalities) on the real and official attitude of the Catholic Church towards non-Catholics, as well as a comment on the following questions:

1. Does your Church claim, or has she ever claimed, the right to punish or persecute dissenters such as lapsed Catholics, Protestants or non-religionists?

2. If your reply is in the negative, how can you explain the frightful religious atrocities of the Inquisition or the harshness of the Church today in Italy and Spain towards Protestants?

Answer:

1. The Church does not claim, nor has she ever claimed the right to punish or persecute religious dissenters because of their beliefs. Her concept of faith as a gift from God and not the mere product of fear, force or theological research should be sufficient proof of this statement.

2. Underlying many of the customs and laws of countries like Spain and Italy is the Catholic philosophy of life. The ordinary citizenry (not the Church) formed in such a philosophy is bound to react harshly against the intrusions of

those whose subjectivistic theology, if not outrightly anti-Catholic, endorses divorce, contraception and euthanasia —ideas that are repugnant to traditional Christian doctrine and discipline.

In Rev. Sheridan's answer to the second question as printed above in "The Tidings" he states that the people, not the Church, reacted harshly to the "intrusions" of the heretics. He does not reconcile this with the bulls of the Popes or the actions of Franciscan and Dominican inquisitors. Rev. Sheridan's evasion of the questions shocked me so much that I wrote him.

May 31, 1956

Rev. John V. Sheridan
% The Tidings
1530 W. 9th Street
Los Angeles, California

Dear Rev. Sheridan:

I have been sent a copy of your column "Question Box" from the Tidings of May 10, 1956. In this issue you state "The Church does not claim nor has she ever claimed, the right to punish or persecute religious dissenters because of their belief."

I am curious to know how you can reconcile this statement with the historical facts of the Inquisition. I used to think, too, that the Inquisition was largely a Spanish phenomenon led by bloodthirsty characters such as Torquemada, but the facts of history belie this whitewashing. Do you remember the Bull "Ad Extirpanda" of Pope Innocent the IV, the authorization of torture and imprisonment for heretics, and the roles of the Dominicans and Franciscans for a long period of time as the official inquisitors for the Holy See? Have you ever read *The History of the Inquisition of the Middle Ages,* by Lea? It presents some fifteen hundred pages of detailed historical fact that is directly the opposite of your statement.

Very sincerely yours,

s/Emmett McLoughlin

His answer:

Catholic Information Center
Our Lady Chapel
809 South Flower Street
Los Angeles, California

June 8, 1956

Mr. Emmett McLoughlin
Superintendent, Memorial Hospital
1200 South Fifth Avenue
Phoenix, Arizona

Dear Mr. McLoughlin:

I am replying to your kind inquiry of May 31st.

It is assumed that you are acquainted with the qualifications for an Ex Cathedra definition on matters of Faith and Morals. There has, in fact, been no such definition claiming for the Church "the right to punish or persecute religious dissenters because of their beliefs" notwithstanding, of course, Innocent's (IV) Ad Extirpanda or some of the shameful inquisitorial practices of his time. My Tidings statement therefore still stands and need not be reconciled with the *disciplinary* practices of any era, however universal or harsh they may seem to us now.

We are, indeed, acquainted with all of Lea's historical works including his earlier *Superstition and Force*—which should give any honest critic a key to what other historians recognize as a biased assemblage of statistics, *A History of the Inquisition of the Middle Ages* and *A History of the Inquisition of Spain*. In this connection, I suggest that you consult Baumgarten's critical and highly documented *Lea's Historical Works*.

Without holding any brief for many of the Inquisitors or "white-washing" some of their unpardonable practices, I think it is only fair to say that Lea was hopelessly lacking in the qualities of a good historian which include not only the elementary ability to collect documents but a sympathetic evaluation of the mood of a milieu. He failed to understand the revolutionary nature of Catharism, the common man's legitimate confusion of treason with heresy, the harsh and disproportionate nature of penalties up to recent time, the terrible political pressure on the medieval popes, the undeveloped legal disciplines, the weaknesses of individual ecclesiastics and the Church's understandable zeal to keep both the Faith and society unsundered by a threat that in medieval times was as terrible as that of Communism today.

If, Emmett, you are honestly interested in matters of this nature I would sincerely suggest that you withdraw yourself, temporarily at least, from the destructive and superficial influence of a climate of thought and a group of individuals that are, frankly, as little at home in the field of scholarly research as the Dead Sea Scrolls in the hands of an African witch doctor.

I would be happy to have you call on me if you are in town and assure you of my earnest prayers.

Cordially and sincerely yours,

s/Rev. John Sheridan
Director

JVS/bjz

The Rev. Sheridan did not tell his public what he wrote in his letter to me; i. e., that the Church in its *disciplinary* action persecuted heretics shamefully. He ignores the fact that the Popes took such action because they believed they had the *right* to persecute heretics. He also forgets that the Church's claimed infallibility extends to "faith and *morals*" and that the persecution, imprisonment and slaughter of dissenters is certainly a matter of *morals.*

According to his Church's teaching, a doctrine such as the *right* to persecute and kill dissenters, must be accepted not only if it be formally promulgated "ex Cathedra" by a Pope, but also if it be the decree of a general council of the Church or if it becomes an accepted doctrine of the "teaching magisterium (authority)" of the Church over a considerable period of time. This fact he furthermore forgets, or ignores. The right to ferret out, investigate, torture, imprison and kill the forerunners of Protestants was taught and carried out for more than four hundred years. That would seem to be a considerable period of time.

Of this whole story of the Inquisition, most Catholics, both students and adults, are told extremely little.

Catholic students are not taught that the spirit of the Inquisition still permeates the Catholic hierarchy. They are not taught that now, in the latter half of the twentieth century, every Roman Catholic bishop in the world, in his Consecration Oath swears to the following: ". . .With all my power I shall track down and attack all heretics, schismatics and those who rebel against the Lord (Pope) and his successors . . . So help me God, and these the holy gospels of God." [8]

Pope Innocent IV wrote his condemnation of heresy in 1198. His decree would assume that heresy existed—

as indeed it had in the eyes of the Catholic hierarchy since the latter's evolution. There had been the Coptics, the Anabaptists, the Monophysites, the Monothelesites, the Manicheans and others of the early Christian centuries. As the centuries passed, the rebellious heresies grew in numbers and frighteningly so in their threat to the papacy. There were the Albigenses, the Wycliffites, the Hussites, the Waldenses, and particularly the Cathari.

The Popes and their bishops felt that these heretics threatened the very existence of the Catholic Church. Hence, the Inquisition. In the light of these historical facts the pamphlet of the Paulist Press, *Come Home Again,* by Rev. Wilfred G. Hurley, seems strange:

History definitely declares that for sixteen hundred years after Christ there was only the Catholic Church. The "Faith of our Fathers" could have been only the Faith of this Catholic Church.

For the oldest non-Catholic Church only goes back for the short space of four hundred years.

Thus from the day of Christ up until three hundred or four hundred years ago, everyone who believed in Christ believed exactly and precisely as the Catholic Church believes and practices today.

Every historian, Catholic, non-Catholic, Jewish or infidel, will tell you that this is so.

The story of the Inquisition, as condensed in the preceding pages of this chapter, is well documented and authentic. It is one of the most important phases of the history of Catholicism, from the viewpoint both of its crucial nature and of the millions of people affected. Yet it is either completely ignored or cursorily glossed over in the textbooks of the Roman Catholic educational system of America.

Catholic parochial pupils are taught that the councils of the Church, both provincial and general, constitute one of the greatest guarantees of the Church's unity and integrity of doctrine. In the Catholic history textbook, *Christianity and Civilization,* the following statement is made: "In maintaining this unity and solving her many problems, the Church received tremendous help from her councils . . . matters relating to the whole Church were taken up by general or ecumenical councils."

We were also taught that, among the general councils, one of the greatest was the Council of Trent. We were taught that some evils existed in the Church in Luther's time; but that Luther, Calvin, Zwingli and the others could not and did not correct them. The true reformation occurred when the bishops voluntarily gathered under the leadership of the Pope. In Council assembled, they re-emphasized all the true doctrines of the Church, purified its hierarchical structure and immeasurably strengthened its discipline.

The following is from *Christianity and Civilization* (pp. 284-285):

Program of Reform. While the Protestant sects were wrecking the spiritual unity of Christendom with their new heresies, the Church was slowly working for a true reformation. Many of the faithful had been urging a reform, which would retain the traditional teaching of the Church and the unity of its organization. "Man must be changed by religion, not religion by men." This reform was achieved within the Church through a program that included (1) a restatement of the true doctrines of Christianity on an authoritative basis, (2) a reorganization of the government and practices of the clergy, and (3) the formation of new monastic orders that taught the Faith with a renewed zeal.

The Council of Trent. The Council of Trent (1545-1563), meeting over nearly a twenty-year period, often interrupted by wars and politics, clarified the teaching of the Church on the issues raised and attacked by the Protestants. It published a catechism in which its stand was clearly defined. It re-affirmed that the Scriptures *and tradition* were the basis of the Catholic religion, and rejected private judgement by re-serving to the Church the right to interpret the Bible. It denied the doctrine of "justification by faith alone" and in-sisted on the necessity of good works. Papal supremacy in the Church and the necessity of the seven sacraments were likewise reaffirmed by the Council.

To eliminate many of the abuses that had developed in the Church, the Council of Trent promulgated long overdue dis-ciplinary statutes. These provided for the establishment of seminaries and required the bishops and other ecclesiastics to live in their own dioceses and to devote themselves to spiritual work. Many of the financial abuses were likewise eliminated. The *Index,* a list of books forbidden to Catholics, was published.

Another "objective" history textbook, the *American History for Catholic High Schools,* says the same thing (p. 19):

Long before Luther's day, good men had been pleading and praying for reforms. In the end, these reforms were brought about not by revolt but by the rallying of forces within the Church. Action toward reform that would have official Church approval was undertaken through the Council of Trent (1545-1563). This general council suppressed existing

evils, enacted special regulations for the training of the
clergy and for the direction of monastic life, and clarified
Catholic doctrine, especially in matters disputed by the
Protestants.

I had accepted this version of the Council of Trent for
many years. It is taught also in advance seminary textbooks. The true story of that Council, which I learned
since leaving the priesthood, was to me one of the most
shocking disillusionments in a violent series of disillusionments regarding the Roman Catholic Church's history,
doctrines, and morals. My authority for my revised picture of the Council of Trent is Henry Charles Lea. Previously I quoted a letter from a Rev. Sheridan of the
"Tidings" in Los Angeles impugning Lea's historical ability and integrity. No priest or ex-priest could honestly
agree with Sheridan after reading Lea's voluminous Latin
footnotes.

To make doubly sure, I verified Lea's reputation with
the University of Pennsylvania. The following is a letter
I received:

University of Pennsylvania
Philadelphia 4

The Library

27 March 1957

Mr. Emmett McLoughlin
Memorial Hospital
1200 S. Fifth Avenue
Phoenix, Arizona

My dear Mr. McLoughlin:

The reputation of Henry Charles Lea is securely guaranteed
by some sixteen scholarly volumes on ecclesiastical history

and institutions. We have now in the Henry Charles Lea Library (located in the Main Library at the University of Pennsylvania) about 17,000 volumes relating to the history of the medieval and early modern Church.

Sincerely yours,
s/Kenneth M. Setton,
Henry C. Lea Professor of History

The names of the Popes, cardinals and, most important, the dates of the convocations and ending of sessions as stated by Lea are confirmed in the Catholic volume *Canons and Decrees of the Council of Trent* by Rev. H. J. Schroeder, O. P. (Dominican), Herder Book Co., St. Louis & London, 1941.

The first point is that the Council of Trent was not convened by Pope Paul III of his own accord. It did not result from the prodding of the hierarchy, but from the insistence of the leaders of Europe, particularly the Emperor Charles V.

The second significant point is that these leaders did not urge a general council for any doctrinal redeclaration. They wanted a moral cleansing of the Church *through the abolition of celibacy and the permission for priests to marry.*

The third point was that the Pope, cardinals and bishops so boycotted the meetings of the Council that it dragged on for years.

The fourth point is that the Council of Trent, in the eyes of its contemporaries, was a complete failure.

The strange fact to a modern Catholic is that the insistence for a universal council to reform the Roman Catholic Church came from the followers of Luther (none of whom wanted to leave the mother Church), the princes and local bishops, particularly German. The opposition to the Council came from the papal court and the high ecclesiastics who were waxing rich over fines and penalties (some payable in advance) for violations of the existing laws, especially the law of celibacy. The Bavarian orator, August Baumgartner, told the Council, when it finally assembled, that ninety-six percent of the Catholic clergy were either openly married or living in concubinage. The Emperor Charles V, the princes and sincere bishops wanted the Council to abolish the unobserved law of clerical celibacy in order to protect the women of the parishes from seduction, particularly through the confessional. They wanted also to interest good normal men in the ministry.

The Vatican court, throughout the Protestant Reformation and a thousand years before, was as debauched as any accused Oriental court. The pressure of Emperor Charles, the Reformers, and the good bishops was to force the Papacy to call a general Council with a hope of reforming the Papal court first, and then the general structure of the entire Church.

The first bone of contention was the location of the Council. The Pope was afraid of a council seat within the German domain. The Emperor distrusted the Pope and any council seat under Italian influence.

In 1536 the Pope suggested Mantua, Italy. The Lutherans and Henry VIII of England objected. At this point, it is obvious that the Reformation was to be a pan-Catholic affair, with all rebels returning to the fold, if a purging of the "mother house" could be effected. The letter of Henry VIII to Charles V (April 8, 1538) is expressive of their mutual distrust of the Pope: "Howe, if he (the Pope) calle us to one of his owne townes, we be afraid to be at suche an hostes table. We saye, Better to ryse a hungred, then to go thense with our bellyes fulle."

Pope Paul III first ordered the opening of the Council on May 17, 1537. It was merely a gesture. No delegates appeared. He transferred the Council to Vincenza, Italy. Still by May 1, 1538, no bishops or cardinals had presented themselves to show any interest in reforming the Church. (Luther had made his break in 1517—twenty-one years before.)

The pressure from the Emperor continued. Four years later (November 22, 1542) Pope Paul III ordered the Council convened at Trent in northern Italy. So few appeared that nothing was done and the Council was suspended in July, 1543. It was convoked again two years later in 1545; but from all Christendom only twenty bishops presented themselves to reform the Roman Church. By the time of the formal opening, December 13, 1545, only five more delegates had arrived.

For fifteen months, this handful of ecclesiastics purported to represent the entire Church and, under the control of the Pope, expounded on dogma and dogmatics and completely ignored the purpose for which the Council had been forced upon them—the reform of the clergy, particularly through the ecclesiastical approval of their unions with the women of their choice through legitimatized marriage. The decrees of these few men succeeded only in erecting an impenetrable doctrinal barrier between the "old" Church and the rising rebellious organizations.

In 1547, the German bishops and the imperial ambassadors continued to press for some action. The Pope transferred the Council to Bologna. Constant adjournments caused universal contempt until it was suspended in 1549.

A new Pope, Julius III, reconvened the council, on May 1, 1551. The Lutheran theologians who had been attending the Council left the assemblage; and, on April 28, 1552, the party broke up again.

Ten years passed. The people continued their pressure for reform, particularly for the legitimate marriage rather than the almost uncontrolled universal concubinage of the clergy—until Pope Pius IV was obliged to reconvene the Council of Trent on January 18, 1562.

A Commission to study reforms recommended that the only possible elimination of the vices existing in the conventual orders (one of them was the Franciscan Order of which I was a member) lay in their abolition. Cardinal Caraffa, who headed the commission, proposed that no new members be permitted, so that these orders could die out. This same commission protested against the facility with which men in holy orders were able to purchase from the Roman Curia dispensations to marry.

The history of the period shows almost frantic efforts of local bishops and devout Catholic rulers to achieve moral reforms, with no cooperation from Rome. The continuing Council of Trent was mere papal diversionary windowdressing.

In 1560, Emperor Ferdinand I asked for a reconvocation of the Council of Trent with legislation permitting marriage of the clergy. The local rulers argued simply that celibacy was so unnatural and impossible that priests did not observe it. The Duke of Cleves stated that, in his sovereignty (a very populous one), there were not five priests without concubines. Ruler after ruler appeared before the Council demanding ecclesiastical marriage as a stabilizing force in Christendom. Emperor Ferdinand argued along the same lines; as did King Charles IX of France.

The Council of Trent ended in 1563. It had done nothing on the issue for which the leaders had sought its assistance in the stabilization of clerical society. The violation of celibacy had been a common fact for fifteen hundred years. It had been a matter of discipline. The Council of Trent made it a matter of doctrine and thereby accentuated guilt for all future centuries.

The Council of Trent was not wanted by the Popes and they did nothing to make it a success. The "heretics" who had tried to reunite the Church in a spelling out of doctrine and a reasonable stabilization of moral concepts gave up. Protestantism became a permanent reality.

Because of the apathy, the opposition and the disinterest of the papal curia and the "top flight" hierarchy, the principal objectives of the Council of Trent: (1) the reconciliation of heretics and (2) the "purification" of the clergy were both failures.

None of this story of the aim and of the failure of the Council of Trent was taught to me in a Catholic high school, or a junior or senior Catholic seminary.

For those interested in its verification I can recommend the *History of Sacerdotal Celibacy in the Christian Church*, pages 442-475.

The story about the Vatican Council and the issuance of the dogma of Papal Infallibility can be more briefly told than that of the Council of Trent.

Catholic children are taught in parochial schools that papal infallibility is grounded in the Bible; that it has always been an accepted segment of Catholic doctrine throughout the world; and that the Vatican Council in 1870, with complete unanimity, had merely confirmed an ancient dogma of Catholicism.

They are not taught that the dogma was "sprung" on the assembled bishops two months after the Council opened; that it was not believed throughout Christian history nor all over the world; and that one hundred bishops representing nearly half the Roman Catholics in the world wrote in protest to the presiding cardinals.

They are not taught that letters were sent to Pope Pius IX by forty-six German and Austrian bishops, forty-one French bishops, and twenty-seven North American bishops (including Purcell of Cincinnati, Kendrick of St. Louis, McCloskey of New York) petitioning that infallibility be removed from the agenda.

Catholic classroom history books do not bring out the fact that, on the day before the vote on papal infallibility, eighty-eight bishops left Rome because they could not conscientiously vote for it; and, because of papal reprisals, dared not vote against it.

They do not tell Catholic children that papal infallibility was purely a political thing rammed down the throats of Catholics by the Pope Pius IX in order to bolster his prestige in a crumbling papal empire. Garibaldi had taken the papal states away from him in the famous "March on Rome."

Parochial history books overlook the fact that the bishops voting for the dogma of papal infallibility were largely the two hundred and seventy-six Italian bishops (dependent on the Pope for their bread as well as their authority) and their Latin kinsmen of Spain and South America.

I was never taught that the dogma was opposed by the bishops and archbishops of Paris, Prague, Vienna, Rottenburg, Mainz, Orleans, Marseilles, Grenoble, Besancon, Dijon, La Rochelle, Halifax, Cincinnati, St. Louis, Pittsburgh, Savannah, Wheeling, Newark, Little Rock, New York, and many others. The details of events concerning the Vatican Council of 1870 can be found in *Under Orders* by William Sullivan, published by Richard Smith in New York.

The greatest mass hypnosis of the Catholic parochial school system concerns the reconciliation of Catholicism with Americanism. It imbues those children with the idea that a good Catholic can be a good American, that the teachings of the Church are not only compatible with the ideals of our Founding Fathers, but that those men— Jefferson, Franklin, Hancock and the rest—secured their ideas which they wrote into the Declaration of Independence from the writings of St. Thomas Aquinas and St. Robert Bellarmine. (*Our Sunday Visitor*, July 3, 1955.)

A vague notion prevails in Catholic schools that true American citizenship is achieved by voting, by obeying the laws, by pledging allegiance to the flag, and by serving in the armed forces.

Our Sunday Visitor headlined in the 1954, July 4th edition, "If You're a Good Catholic, You're a Good American." Its story emphasizes that the "self evident" truths and rights of Americans were denied in countries that did not believe in God (obviously Communistic) and that, since Catholics believe in God, they are good Americans.

The Arizona REGISTER (August 26, 1955) editorialized:

Could it be perhaps that Catholics have not sufficiently advertised the patriotic side of parochial education? If that is what the opposition fears about Catholic education, the answers have been given. As much was recorded by the National Catholic Educational Association earlier this year. Spokesman was Archbishop Leo Binz of Iowa, who declared, "In the total picture of our philosophy of education, patriotism looms large as one of the strongest arguments in favor of religious schools . . ."

Seconding the stand, the entire delegation of 12,000 priests, nuns, and brothers from all parts of the nation pledged themselves to intensify their effort to serve our nation *under God* through the schools.

The phrase "under God" is reminiscent of the words frequently found on the cornerstones of Catholic schools *Pro Deo et Patria* (For God and Country). The difficulty around the world has been that "God" is identified with the Catholic Church and its hierarchy and therefore when crises have arisen "country" comes second.

There is no concept taught in parochial schools that democracy is established upon *principles* and that the *acknowledgment and preservation of those principles are vital to the preservation of American democracy*—and our nation as we now know it and might wish to keep it. The

principles upon which American democracy is founded
are absolutely rejected by the Roman Catholic Church.
This fact is concealed from American parochial school
children and is not even realized by most of the Roman
clergy.

The acknowledged foundations of the United States
of America are (1) freedom of individual thought; (2)
freedom of worship; (3) separation of church and state;
(4) government drawing its authority from the consent
of the governed.

The freedom of the human mind is fundamental in
America. Freedom to think as one pleases, freedom to
read, to discuss, to argue, to take any side on any matter
of philosophy, science or theology are among the self-
evident rights of Americans.

Although Catholic students do not know it, freedom
of thought is formally condemned by the highest authorities of the Roman Catholic Church.

Before quoting the decrees of Popes, it might be well
to re-emphasize Roman Catholic doctrine regarding infallibility. This divine immunity from doctrinal and moral
error is threefold. It is taught to rest upon the Pope personally when he officially defines a doctrine "ex-cathedra";
upon the General Councils of the Church; and upon the
"teaching magisterium" or teaching authority of the
Church. The Pope is the head of that authority. When he
teaches doctrines or defines morals, as Popes are accustomed to do in encyclicals and allocutions, he speaks as
the head of the universal teaching "magisterium" and
Catholics must assent. They are, at least, "suspect of
heresy" if they deny them.

Therefore, Catholic parochial school children in the

twentieth century accept and adhere to the declarations of the Popes, regardless of the century or year they were proclaimed.

Pope Gregory XVI in his encyclical against "modernism" (*Mirari vos arbitramur*, August 15, 1832) said: "And from this most putrid spring of indifference flows that absurd and erroneous opinion or rather insanity that teaches and upholds that everyone should have freedom of thought." [9]

Freedom of thought was also condemned by Pope Pius IX (*Gravissimas Inter*) December 11, 1862, and by Pope Leo XIII (*Immortale Dei*, November 1, 1885.) In 1888, this same Pope wrote, "By no means is it permissible to seek or to defend or to grant freedom of thought, freedom of instruction, freedom of writing . . . as rights granted to man by nature." [10]

The Index of Forbidden Books, banning books, not only by specific titles and authors, but by whole broad categories, is the strongest objective proof that the Roman hierarchy must try to destroy that American cornerstone of freedom of thought.

The American concept of freedom of worship and free choice of religion is the natural flowering of freedom of thought. America's history begins with the tales of peoples fleeing from Europe specifically for the purpose of worshiping God as they wished—not as they were told. The story of our early days passes on the monuments of the Congregationalists and the Unitarians of New England, the Quakers in Pennsylvania and the Catholics in Florida.

Religious liberty is of the essence of the American way of life. The great cathedrals of the east, the revival tents of the southwest, the ivy covered churches of our large cities, the chapels of the plains, the great Mormon temple of Utah, the Jewish synagogues everywhere, the Chautauqua, the sawdust trails, the Four Square Gospel, are as important to America as are the Declaration of Independence, the Golden Gate, the Grand Canyon, the Texas Panhandle or the Statue of Liberty. The Constitution of the United States guarantees their freedom.

But the Catholic Church condemns that freedom and, if it could, it would destroy it. Every American priest in his profession of faith condemns this freedom of worship upon which America is founded.

"I accept without hesitation, and profess all that has been handed down, defined and declared by the Sacred Canons and by the General Councils . . . at the same time I condemn and reprove all that the Church has condemned and reproved."

Pope Clement VIII (in the early 17th century) condemned the famous Edict of Nantes, which granted freedom of worship, as "the most accursed thing that can be imagined, whereby liberty of conscience (or freedom of worship) is granted to everybody, which is the worst thing in the world."

The American concept of freedom of worship is also indirectly but very effectively condemned by the Roman Catholic Church's insistence that it alone is the true Church of God, that it alone can lead men to heaven, and that all those outside its fold, except morons and stupid savages, are doomed to hell.

Since the Roman Catholic Church is still a minority group in the United States, it thrives through the sufferance and tolerance of the Protestant majority. So the politic thing is for it, too, to be tolerant of Protestants. Occasionally some over-zealous priest (Father Feeney in Boston) or a non-Catholic disinters the old skeleton— *Extra ecclesium nulla salus.* (Outside the Church there is no salvation)—and the theologians are sore put to explain away one of their strongest doctrines.

American parochial school children are shocked when their non-Catholic neighbors tell them that Catholicism damns everyone else to hell. They want reassurance from their priests; and they get it. They are told that God judges everyone according to his own lights, that even though the Catholic Church is the only true Church, a sincere Baptist or Methodist or Presbyterian may be saved because of his ignorance. If he is sincere in that ignorance, he belongs to the "soul of the Church." That may be a reassuring, tolerant doctrine to a parochial school pupil; but it is not Roman Catholic doctrine.

The Roman Church cannot change its principle that it alone offers salvation; and the escape hatch of the "soul of the Church" embraces only those who are "invincibly" or moronically ignorant.

As early as 585 A.D., Pope Pelagius II (*Quod ad dilectioneum*) condemned as "damned and anathematized" anyone who "thought or believed or dared to teach" the contrary.

On December 18, 1208, Pope Innocent III ordered as a Profession of Faith for converted Waldensians, "We believe with our hearts and profess with our lips one holy, Roman, Catholic, and apostolic, outside of which we believe no one can be saved."

The Ecumenical (universal) Council of the Lateran decreed in 1215: "There is indeed only one universal

Church for the faithful outside of which by no means can anyone be saved."

The doctrine was reiterated by Pope Boniface VIII (Bull *Unam Sanctam,* November 18, 1302) and Pope Clement VI (Bull *Super Quibusdam,* September 29, 1351). The Ecumenical Council of Florence, under Pope Eugene IV, declared on February 4, 1442: "The Roman Church, the voice of our Lord and Savior . . . firmly believes, professes and preaches that no one not within the Catholic Church, not only pagans, but Jews and heretics and schismatics, can participate in eternal life but are destined for eternal hell fire 'which was prepared for the Devil and his angels.' "

This same monopoly on heaven is taught by the official Profession of Faith of the Council of Trent (confirmed by the Bull of Pope Pius IV, *Injunctum Nobis,* November 13, 1564). It is repeated by Pope Benedict XIV, *Nuper ad Nos,* March 16, 1743; Pope Gregory XVI, *Mirari Vos Arbitramur,* August 15, 1832; Pope Pius IX, *Singulari Quadam,* December 9, 1854, *Quanto Conficiamur Moerore,* August 10, 1863, and the Syllabus of Errors, 1864; Pope Leo XIII, *Satis Cognitum,* June 29, 1896; and Pope Pius XII, *Humani Generis,* August 12, 1950.

The Profession of Faith now in use contains the words, "this same Catholic Faith, outside of which nobody can be saved . . . ," (*Priest's New Ritual,* P. J. Kennedy & Sons, N. Y., 1947, p. 52 b.). The Official Baltimore Catechism No. 3, approved by Cardinal Spellman (Benziger Brothers, N. Y.), has as question No. 412, "Are all obliged to belong to the Catholic Church in order to be saved?" and the answer: "All are obliged to belong to the Catholic Church in order to be saved." The traditional Deharbe's

Large Catechism (Benziger Brothers, N. Y., 1921) has question No. 33, "Why is the Catholic Church called the 'only saving' church? Because she alone was established by Christ and commissioned to save men's souls."

The famous Roman Catholic apologist, Philip, frankly states the hierarchy's position. He is quoted in *Converted Catholic,* January, 1953, as follows:

The Church (Roman) rejects the principle of free investigation which makes reason the judge over God's utterances and over her own teaching office; she knows herself as the only true Church, and cannot recognize Protestantism as another equally legitimate form of Christianity . . . She rejects in principle the freedom of all worships. Freedom of worship is in itself an evil.

Not only does Catholicism teach that men cannot be saved through non-Catholic churches. Its leaders have sworn to destroy those churches. Every Roman Catholic bishop, upon his consecration, takes an oath of allegiance to the Pope. It contains these words:

"With all my power I shall persecute and make war upon all heretics, schismatics and those who rebel against our lord (the Pope) and all his successors . . . So help me God and these the holy gospels of God."[11]

The important word in this oath is "heretics." The term "heretic" is defined in Roman Canon Law, Canon 1325 No. 2, "A heretic is any baptized Christian who stubbornly doubts or denies any truths of the divine and Catholic faith." This includes all Baptists, Methodists, Presbyterians, Mormons, Episcopalians, Lutherans, and every other non-Roman Catholic Christian group.

An American Catholic parochial school youngster should revolt at the thought of his American Catholic bishop making physical and political war upon his non-Catholic playmate next door. But that is what his bishop has sworn to do; and that is what his fellow bishops in Catholic countries are now doing.

The founders of America—Jefferson, Franklin, Washington, Hancock, Hamilton—seem to have been almost inspired by God in their wisdom. They were also careful students of European history. Too often they had seen priesthoods throughout the centuries drag countries into destroying wars by using the state as their avenging arm. Too often, too, they had seen emperors and kings buy off Popes, or intimidate patriarchs and, by the state control of religion, prostitute God in politics.

They wanted none of it. They were afraid that, in their first enthusiastic expressions of liberty, there might have been loopholes. They plugged them with the first words of the Bill of Rights: "Congress shall make no law respecting an establishment of religion." In other words—complete separation of church and state.

The struggle of church and state for power over each other had plagued the Egyptians, the Assyrians, the Macedonians, the Jews, the Greeks and the Romans. Its see-saw control runs through the migration of nations. As the countries of Europe were born, the battle went on, with the only satisfactory temporary compromise reached in the Holy Roman Empire of Charlemagne.

Ours is the first nation in the history of civilization to solve the problem and cut the Gordian knot by pushing the adversaries apart and forcing them to stay apart.

But the American solution does not satisfy the Roman Catholic Church. Its officials realize that, so long as complete separation of church and state exists, it cannot control America. And it must try to control the moral life of America. Therefore, it condemns the American separation of church and state.

Pope Gregory XVI took cognizance of the new American doctrine and formally condemned it in 1832.

Pope Pius IX in 1864 condemned as item 55 among the errors of society the principle "that the church should be separated from the state and the state from the church."[12]

This rejection of the first amendment to the American Constitution was repeated by Pope Leo XIII in 1885 and by Pope Pius X in 1906. It was characterized as a "violation of justice . . . an offense against the dignity of the Holy See and the person of the Pope." (Encyclical *Vehementer Nos*, Feb. 11, 1906).[13]

As recently as November 3, 1954, Pope Pius XII repudiated the principle of separation of church and state and reasserted the ancient papal claim of vicarious divine sovereignty by telling forty cardinals and two hundred and five bishops that the Catholic Church's jurisdiction "cannot be limited to . . . things 'strictly religious'" but extends to "the moral aspect of all law."[14]

Every law is adopted for the sole purpose of governing men's actions or morals. Therefore, the Pope now, in our day and time, claims a veto power over all the earth's parliaments and congresses, while his American hierarchy acclaims "the principle of separation of church and state, to which we fully subscribe."[15]

Our Declaration of Independence, among the truths which it holds to be self-evident—and which everyone claiming American citizenship, even Catholic priests, must approve—declares that governments are instituted among *men,* deriving their just powers from *the consent of the governed.*

The Roman Catholic Church has always taught the "divine right of kings," but it has taught that that right came through the Pope. The heads of the Roman Church have enforced the fealty of peoples, have absolved nations from loyalty to their rulers and have tossed whole countries to kings and emperors as they would bones to a dog.

The claims of some medieval Popes, as the source of civil government, sound like the rantings of petulant lunatics.

Pope Boniface VIII (*Unam sanctam,* November 18, 1302), swollen with the thought of his own infallibility, thundered: "We declare, state and define and pronounce that to obtain salvation every human creature must be subject to the Roman pontiff . . . In his power there are two swords, the spiritual and the temporal—and both are under the power of the Church."[16]

Pope Gregory VII wrote "the Pope alone is able to bind and to lose, to give and to take away . . . empires, kingdoms, duchies, countships and the possessions of all men."

Pope Alexander VIII made the same presumptuous claim in 1690 (*Inter multiplices*).[17]

Recent Popes have not repudiated the pretenses of their predecessors that all power of civil government throughout the world comes from God solely through the papacy.

Popes Pius IX and Leo XIII have emphatically re-emphasized it.

Pope Pius IX in 1864 declared that the Catholic Church must exercise power "not only over all individual men but also over nations, peoples and their rulers." We might wonder how Abraham Lincoln felt about this decree, if he heard about it, as he was leading the United States through the Civil War.

A few years after our Civil War, as our people were readjusting to the concept of Thomas Jefferson that the power to govern came from the people, Pope Leo XIII re-emphasized in 1885: "The source of governmental power comes from God alone. It does not come from the people."

Pope John XXIII still wears the tiara, the triple crown, claiming threefold authority, even if he can't exercise it, conferred with the words, "Thou art the father of Princes and Kings, the *Ruler of the World,* and the Vicar of Jesus Christ."

Our founders believed that, if the people delegated the power to rule over them, the people could take it away. Our Declaration of Independence says: "Whenever any form of government becomes destructive of these ends, it is the right of the people to alter or abolish it." Pope Pius IX condemned this cornerstone of Americanism in his syllabus by denying any circumstances under which it is "lawful to withhold obedience from established rulers, much less to rebel against them."

These basic, fundamental, irreconcilable conflicts and divergencies between the ideals of American democracy and the decrees of the *magisterium,* ultimate papal teaching authority of Catholicism, were never emphasized to me, during twenty-one years of Catholic education. I was taught all of these doctrines, particularly that there was no salvation outside the Catholic Church. But no priest or nun ever compared them to the Declaration of Independence or the Constitution of the United States.

CHAPTER SEVEN

Malignancy of Censorship

The printed and spoken word and their control constitute another "classroom" as effective in the "education" of young and less young Roman Catholics as any physical school building under the hierarchy's jurisdiction.

American Catholic parochial school children, unless they learn to think for themselves and rebel, are isolated from any present day activities or teachings of their hierarchy that would either embarrass them before their American neighbors or possibly make them realize how anachronous their Church is in a modern world. The average good Catholic pupil, or adult for that matter, sees only what his Church wants him to see: the local parish, the local clergy, the nearest Catholic hospital, the liturgy. All the rest goes on behind the "silken curtain" of vestment and ritual; or is kept from him through censorship.

We were taught in the parochial school, as well as in the seminary, that the Roman Catholic faith was the only one that thrived in the metropolises of the world (and particularly in America) in the face of sin, of materialism and of godlessness—because it alone was of God.

We were taught that in the Near East and the Orient the pagan cults of Mohammedanism, Shintoism and Hinduism survived because the civilization around them was as archaic and unchallenging as themselves. In America, we were told, the Mennonites sought the protection of the backwoods; the Mormons thrived only in Utah and the farming areas of surrounding states; and the Baptists held their strength in illiterate communities of the deep South.

Our priests neglected to point out that the Mormons, the Methodists and the Baptists increase and multiply, even though their children are subjected to all the cross-currents of thought and opinion of the public schools.

Catholic children retain their faith and their outlook because their parochial school system and its adjunct media of indoctrination and mental protection try to isolate them from competitive American thought.

Before the era of modern communication and information—the press, radio, motion pictures and television—this isolation was relatively simple. The *Index of Forbidden Books* was enough. As these other media developed, the hierarchy has felt it necessary to try to control them, too.

It does this to protect its children, in school and out of school. To counteract the "godlessness" of the public press, it has established its own system of newspapers and magazines, with a combined weekly circulation of nearly four million.

But it cannot keep its children from exposure to other means of communication—the daily press, radio, television, phonograph records, motion pictures and the nation's great magazines. So it must try to control them, too, in their presentation of news or of opinion or of history.

It must encourage these media to emphasize and spotlight all news and events favorable to it and to minimize or suppress all happenings or opinions unfavorable to it.

The hierarchy has been so outstandingly successful in this control that there is less truth told and known about the Roman Catholic Church, its doctrines, its history, its contemporary world-wide maneuvers than any other modern phenomenon. Its threats of and actual use of economic boycott backed up by the illusion of a purchasing bloc of some forty million devout Catholics (there are not more than twenty million in the United States—and only a fraction of them are devout) have cowed American editors and publishers and broadcasters who otherwise boast of "the freedom of the press."

The most effective whip for the control of the Catholic pupil's mind is still the *Index of Forbidden Books.* It forbids all Catholics to read any book critical of the hierarchy's doctrines or history or policies. This means that, in the parochial school, the youngsters will never see any textbook or reference book that is critical of the faith or its leaders. Very few pupils desire learning to the point where they seek out additional textbooks in a public library. If they do, they may find that Roman censorship controls the public libraries too.

It even forbids the Bible, unless the Catholic Church has approved the edition.

The Jesuit priest, John J. Lynch, defends the *Index* and other Roman Catholic mental controls in the March, 1957, issue of the Catholic magazine, *Books on Trial.* As we read his words, we should remember that he is a Catholic teacher in a Catholic Jesuit school, Weston College, Weston, Massachusetts. We might wonder how he can reconcile his words with the basic American principles of freedom of thought, of speech and of worship. How do he and the other thousands of priests and nuns answer the questions of those among their four million pupils who are just as proud of being American as being Catholic? Hear Father Lynch:

It is common knowledge that the Catholic Church forbids her members to read certain types of literature which she judges would be a threat to faith or morals. . . .

The point of departure for any intelligent discussion of this question among Catholics is the established fact that the Church is divinely instituted, vested with full right to teach authoritatively and to rule in matters religious, and charged by Christ Himself with the responsibility of safeguarding Catholic faith and morals. In these matters the voice of the Church is the voice of God and commands the same unquestioning obedience which is due the word of God Himself.

. . . In all reasonableness we must concede the right and duty of the church, if she deems it necessary, to exercise a measure of control over the literature which Catholics read and to establish norms and regulations whereby the faith and morals of her subjects will be protected from what we might call "subversive influences." Neither her authority in that sphere, nor her essential wisdom in the exercise of that authority, can be validly questioned once we face the fact of her institution by God as official and authoritative custodian of faith and morals . . .

Scientific scholarship, if exercised competently, objectively and without bias, will never contradict the scriptural teaching of the Church. (italics author's)

For the laity in general it is the bishop of a given territory who may grant, either personally or through a delegate, permission to read literature which is otherwise forbidden. . . . But unless he has acquired special powers beyond those which the Code concedes him directly, even the bishop may give that permission only to specified individuals and for specified titles. He could not, for example, allow "all Catholic graduate students at X University to read whatever may be prescribed in their respective courses." Those who request permissions under this law will find that the chancery requires the names of those who want the permission, the titles of those works which they wish to read, and the reason which makes that reading necessary.

Permission to read forbidden matter is granted with the express understanding that adequate precautions will be taken to prevent the literature in question from falling into the hands of others unauthorized to read it. And no permission, however broad, can ever release us from the obligation under natural law to protect ourselves from danger. None of us is confirmed in grace simply by complying with the requisites of positive law. It may happen that one's own theological background is not always sufficient to solve every difficulty alleged against our faith and to dispel all doubts which may be lodged against our religious convictions. One's first and urgent obligation in that case is to seek explanation and enlightenment from some other who is qualified to expose the error behind the doubt. And it may sometimes happen that decision to abandon that type of reading will prove a prudent additional course of action.

Admittedly there are times when ecclesiastical restrictions on reading impose a considerable inconvenience, perhaps even handicap, upon Catholic scholars. Unfortunately that sometimes is an unavoidable incidental by-product of Church legislation in this regard. But we simply must recognize and respect the fact that the direct intent of these laws, formulated in obedience to Christ's own mandate to His Church, is the protection of the faithful as a whole in the essentials of faith and morals. If the individual good of a comparative few must occasionally suffer, it does so out of deference to the greater good.

Published with ecclesiastical approval.

The above was not a question from the decrees of the Council of Trent which established the *Index of Forbidden Books* in the 16th Century but from a magazine published in March, 1957, as a guide for teachers, teaching American children how to think in American schools— Roman Catholic, that is.

A doctor on our hospital's attending medical staff, now practicing in Phoenix, told me a clever trick he observed that preserved the spirit of the *Index* and still enabled the hierarchy to boast of Catholic freedom of thought. He, a Protestant, was sent to Notre Dame University during the war on an officers' training assignment. The courses were easy and time was so plentiful that he decided to read. He went to the University library and asked the clerk for Erasmus' *In Praise of Folly*. She checked the files, assured him of its availability and went to get the book. She returned and sheepishly told him that the University had it only in French. He told her to get it. He knew French.

Erasmus, the 16th century Dutch priest, severely condemned the Roman Catholic Church and, although he was never formally excommunicated, died outside the fold.

The doctor's curiosity was aroused. He compiled a list of condemned books on philosophy and theology and requested them. Notre Dame University had them all; but none in the English language.

One way of insuring that Catholic students cannot read forbidden books is to forbid them to attend classes in schools where such books are used. This was the action reported in the New York TIMES, September 3, 1956, as being taken by the Roman Bishop Mark Carroll of Wichita, Kansas, in forbidding Catholics to attend some classes in non-Catholic schools.

Bishop Mark K. Carroll, head of the diocese, has charged that many of these courses constitute a form of "brainwashing" that endangers a student's faith in his church and his loyalty to his country.

In a recent pastoral letter, Bishop Carroll directed all Roman Catholic youths in his diocese who were planning to enter non-Catholic colleges anywhere to discuss their educational plans with the local pastors and, in many instances, with the bishop himself.

"I have done this with the specific purpose of warning them against certain courses which are inimicable to their patriotism and faith," he said today in an interview.

"Here at home we have a very sneaky, sly form of brainwashing going on in our secular colleges," he declared. "It is not approved by the boards of regents or by the college presidents. But it is due to individual professors of psychology and philosophy in particular, as well as some professors of sociology, history and economics."

The advice he has given to those students who have conferred with him depended on the individual's age, his background and the curriculum he wished to follow, Bishop Carroll said. A few of the more mature students "who could separate the wheat from the chaff" would be free to take courses in psychology and philosophy or in history and sociology that might otherwise be objectionable, he asserted.

Bishop Carroll was asked what his attitude would be if it were necessary for a young Roman Catholic student to take a course in beginning psychology or philosophy in order to win a degree.

"That would be too bad," he replied. "My answer would probably be 'no.' There are some psychology and philosophy courses that Roman Catholics would fail anyway because they could not write a passing test paper and remain true to their religious teachings."

An American subsidiary of the Roman *Index*, designed to operate with modern speed, is the N. O. D. L. (National Organization for Decent Literature). It not only tells Catholics, especially students, what publications not to read but it tries to see to it that nobody, Catholic, Jew or Protestant, shall read them, by stopping their publication if possible and, if not, by boycotting outlets that sell them.

Many Protestants, especially business men, who boast of their tolerance, seem to symbolically brush off the Roman Catholic Church's controls over its own people by saying: "Why should I worry if the Catholic priests tell their people they cannot eat meat on Friday? It will be time to worry when they close the markets so that I can't get meat on Friday."

It might be well for these well meaning and tolerant Protestants to check to see if their mental "meat markets" are not already being closed.

James Rorty in *Pocket Books* shows how the Roman hierarchy is trying to saddle the Roman *Index of Forbidden Books* on all reading Americans, both Catholic and otherwise.

The N. O. D. L. assumes the prerogative of speaking for all America in censoring publications; but nationally it is exclusively a Roman Catholic body. Its published aim is one that all respectable Americans would have to approve—the elimination or prevention of books that glorify crime, pornography or immorality. But, behind this acceptable front, it acts to condemn or prevent the republication in pocket book form of any book unacceptable to the Roman Church.

The N. O. D. L. was organized in 1937 by a group of Roman Catholic bishops. The censoring board, passing judgments on publications ranging from comic books to the works of Ernest Hemingway and Somerset Maugham, consists of a hundred housewives recruited by the Chicago Council of Catholic Women.

The choice of these women is not guided by any norm of education or experience. They are not even required to read a whole book to condemn it.

The success of N. O. D. L. shows how an organized religious minority group can, to a disturbing extent, "burn books" in a democracy.

"Tolerant" Protestants might think N. O. D. L. censorship is as harmless to their freedom as the fulmination of a parish priest concerning a movie currently showing at a neighboring theatre. The Protestant is still free to see it. However, N. O. D. L. has been as successful as the Legion of Decency in preventing material "unacceptable" to Catholics from being even available to Protestants.

The N. O. D. L. has, through the National Council of Catholic Women, been able to set up local committees for "better" literature. Other faiths are drawn in. So are P. T. A.'s, unions, police departments and local drugstores and newsstands. The national N. O. D. L. list of condemned books is furnished, with the result that even Protestants and Jews throw their weight into campaigns to prevent the sale of books condemned by one hundred Catholic housewives of Chicago.

The method of "block by block" suppression is described by Rorty:

An instruction and procedure sheet issued by the American Council of Catholic Women advises its local A.C.C.W. "decency crusaders" to work closely with the pastor of the parish. Every establishment selling comic books, magazines, or pocket books is visited every two weeks by teams of two or three women. The owner of the store is presented with a copy of the N.O.D.L. list and told that his visitors will be back in two weeks to check the contents of his racks. If the dealer refuses to remove the "disapproved" items, the visitors are instructed not to argue but to report his refusal to their pastor.

Newsdealers and drugstore proprietors are asked to sign pledges to cooperate with the censoring organization; those who comply are provided with copies of the monthly N.O.D.L. lists. In Brooklyn, where in 1955 sixteen "area campaigns" were in progress under the direction of the "Citizens of Brooklyn United for Decent Literature," dealers. . . .

Last Spring the Mohawk Valley (New York) Pharmacists' Association yielded to the pressure of the N.O.D.L. and agreed to take from the news stands some five hundred and thirty comic books, periodicals and paper-backed volumes. Included in the prohibited reading matter were books by Hemingway, Emile Zola, William Faulkner, Lillian Smith and James Jones. Offending works of these authors included *To Have and Have Not, Nana, Sanctuary, Strange Fruit* and *From Here to Eternity.*

In September, 1955, the Baltimore Pharmacists' Association reprinted the N.O.D.L. "Objectionable" list and advised its members not to purchase pocket books so listed. Subsequently two of the major drug chains in the city took the suggested action.

This procedure has gradually spread across the country to the extent that those who cherish freedom of the press have finally become alarmed.

Along with a good deal of more or less salacious trash, most of it issued by pocket houses who are not members of the American Book Publishers' Council, the N.O.D.L.'s disapproved lists include at least three books apiece by W. Somerset Maugham, Emile Zola, John O'Hara, Pierre Louys, Erskine Caldwell, James T. Farrell and James M. Cain; also Nelson Algren's *The Man with the Golden Arm* and *Never Come Morning,* Niven Busch's *Duel in the Sun,* C. S. Forester's *The African Queen,* Ernest Hemingway's *A Farewell to Arms,* D. H. Lawrence's *Lady Chatterley's Lover* and *Love Among the Haystacks,* James A. Michener's *Tales of the South Pacific,* Christopher Morley's *Kitty Foyle,* Irwin Shaw's *The Young Lions,* Natalie Anderson Scott's *The Story of Mrs. Murphy,* and Ben Ames Williams' *The Strange Woman;* also Flaubert's *Madame Bovary,* and a collection of stories by de Maupassant. Among the books designated as "particularly objectionable" by the Detroit N.O.D.L. list were Walter Karig's *Caroline Hicks,* Francois Mauriac's *The Desert of Love,* John Dos

Passos' *The Forty-Second Parallel*, John Masters' *Nightrunners of Bengal*, Vardis Fischer's *Passions Spin the Plot*, Edgar Mittelholzer's *Shadows Move Among Them*, and F. Van Wyck Mason's *Three Harbors*. Parents who think their adolescent children would benefit by reading such books as *The Sexual Side of Marriage* by M. J. Exner, M. D., *How Shall I Tell My Child*, by Belle S. Mooney, and *The Story of My Psychoanalysis*, by John Knight, are unable to buy them in pocket editions where the N.O.D.L. censorship is effective.

The 1956 summer listing of the N. O. D. L. condemned three hundred and seventy-one books. Among them was *Diary of a Nun*. One can imagine how easily my *People's Padre* or this book could slip through the censorship.

It may be that, in pushing the N. O. D. L. for the mental control of Catholics by mentally hamstringing everybody, the American Roman hierarchy has over-played its hand and shown its true attitude toward the freedom of thought and of reading that are of the essence of American democracy.

The American Civil Liberties Union in May, 1957, unlimbered its heaviest artillery against the N. O. D. L. It charged, as a fundamental objection to the N. O. D. L., that "the judgment of a particular group is being imposed upon the freedom of choice of the whole community."

The *ACLU Newsletter* of June, 1957, reported the ACLU statement:

"The N.O.D.L.," it said, "has prepared blacklists, threatened imposed general boycotts and awarded unofficial certificates of compliance." The main pressure is on individual bookstores, drug stores and tobacconists; but, in many cases, police, prosecuting attorneys and military commanders on Army posts have issued orders that no book on the N.O.D.L. list should be sold in their jurisdiction.

The statement closed by saying that the Union "intends to expose in every way it can the use of lists of books as tools of general boycott, and to intervene on behalf of writers, publishers, vendors and purchasers who have the will to explore legal avenues for the maintenance of their freedom."

The ACLU statement was signed by more than one hundred and fifty prominent figures in the fields of publishing and the arts—among them publishers Alfred A. Knopf and M. Lincoln Schuster, critics Lewis Gannett and Lionel Trilling, and authors Carl Carmer, Walter Van Tilburg Clark, Upton Sinclair, Mark Van Doren and William Carlos Williams. Reinhold Niebuhr and Eleanor Roosevelt also signed the document.

One of the rather ridiculous extents to which Catholic censorship, for the protection of youth, will go is the attempted control of recorded music.

One Father Gabriel Hafford of Wisconsin, the spiritual director of the major seminary of the Milwaukee Archdiocese, Professor of Homiletics and Liturgy, has set himself up as the disc jockeys' czar. The story is told in *The Grail* (July, 1954), a Benedictine Order magazine. "Father Hafford's dream (under the slogan 'Decent Discs and Suitable Songs') for his apostolate is that one day all the Catholic teen-age people in the country will recognize the pressure they could put on the record industry and clean it up. 'We could present a boycotting power,' he said, 'that could control even the Hit Parade.'"

His threats have been so effective that the major record companies now kneel at his feet. "New releases are rushed to his door air mail express at the rate of fifty or so a week." His norm for approving a recording, "If there is nothing in a lyric that the kids cannot act out in their own lives, without having to tell it in confession, then it is O. K." On this basis about one-third of the music he auditions is rejected.

Not so ludicrous is the Roman Catholic control of motion pictures through the Roman Catholic "Legion of Decency."

This is so firmly established that there is hardly need for its discussion. The Legion of Decency's tentacles reach into the preproduction planning of films, their bank financing, their production, their advertising and their showing.

When I left the priesthood, a Hollywood firm planned a motion picture of my break with Rome. I was informed that the Catholic representative on the Hayes Committee simply forbade any studio to make a picture regarding me. The order stuck.

After the release of my book *People's Padre,* a Hollywood producer became very enthusiastic about filming the story. When he came to Phoenix to discuss details, he told me that the picture could not be made in Hollywood because of Roman Catholic control there. It would have to be done, he said, in the strictest secrecy because the Catholic Church would go so far as to blow up or set fire to the studio making the picture.

I had often wondered why the magnificent film "Martin Luther" was made in West Germany and not in Hollywood. After talking to the producer who wants to film my life, I think I know.

A Protestant minister told me that he had been told that the "legitimate" motion picture producers were under pressure to present Catholicism in a favorable light by throwing in Catholic scenes, such as weddings, funerals or priestly counseling wherever possible. The minister decided to check for himself. In Los Angeles within one week he viewed, at random, twenty-two full length films. Seventeen of these had scenes that he felt were Catholic propaganda. Many such scenes seemed deliberately dragged in and out of context.

The usual method of Catholic motion picture censorship is to publish lists in diocesan papers listing pictures as A (approved), B (approved for adults only) and C (condemned). Catholics are presumed to be loyal and docile enough to refrain from going to "C" pictures. Protestants cannot find too much fault with this pressure on the Catholic people except to wonder how those people fail to see the inconsistency between this mental straitjacketing and the freedom of speech and thought that are essential to American democracy. The Legion of Decency list in the Arizona REGISTER (July 5, 1957) condemned one hundred and sixty-four current films.

But the easy-going, mentally lazy American Protestant should become belligerent when the Catholic hierarchy tries to bankrupt and close a theatre when it shows a picture which it, the hierarchy, doesn't like.

All Americans are familiar with many produced films over which Francis Cardinal Spellman and his subordinates have become frantic. There have been "The Miracle," "Martin Luther," "The Moon is Blue," and, in 1957, "Baby Doll." Spellman started the obedient chain reaction of subservient episcopal condemnation by banning the film without even having seen it.

The New York TIMES (December 30, 1956) tells that the Bishop of Albany, New York, The Most Reverend William A. Scully, ordered all Catholics to punish the

Strand Theatre of that city by boycotting it for six months for daring to show the condemned film.

This from the New York TIMES:

In his statement, Bishop Scully declared:

"The Stanley-Warner Corporation . . . has adopted the policy showing condemned motion pictures. We, therefore, forbid all Catholics to attend any picture in this theatre during the period of six months.

"The ban is placed also upon all Stanley-Warner theatres in the Diocese of Albany which show the condemned picture 'Baby Doll.' . . ."

Cardinal Spellman of New York has told members of his archdiocese not to see the film under "pain of sin."

A few thinking sincere Catholics are disturbed by this recrudescence of the ancient punishment of the medieval inquisition in a twentieth century democracy. John Cogley, a regular contributor to the lay Catholic *Commonweal*, wrote February 1, 1957:

Presumably, the films to be shown at the boycotted theatre during the period its owner is being punished will be morally acceptable. There is no question then of avoiding the occasion of sin. The purpose is to teach the theatre-owner a lesson and to convince him, by striking at his pocketbook, that he should not exhibit films like "Baby Doll" in the future.

One can not avoid the conclusion that here is a case of naked economic pressure, a display of sheer power. If there were only a few Catholics among the theatre's patrons, the quarantine would be a fruitless gesture. But there are enough to make Catholic disapproval hurt keenly, maybe even fatally. The diocese, it seems, has declared war, with the price of admission the chief weapon.

Several things about this are disturbing, not the least being the candid use of non-spiritual power to achieve a worthy spiritual goal. In the long run, the flourishing of such power never works out well for the Church. There are chapters and chapters of Church history to bear out the contention that in the end the Church loses much more than she gains. Battles are won while wars are lost. The Church, seeming not to trust in her own strength, reaches out for the secular sword—in this case the economic weapon. Then she has to step down to the level of worldly struggle and looks suspiciously like any other power center. . . .

The world has changed radically since spiritual authority was wont to turn to the "secular arm" for support. In our society economic strength is the rough equivalent of the Inquisitional power.

All this may be, and has been, reasonably challenged. I mention it only to point up the fact that Catholics who disapprove of economic sanctions applied by the Church—and many, many do—are not indifferent to public decency. They are concerned about their Church. They do not like to see it regarded as just one more pressure organization flexing its muscles. . . .

Roman Catholic controls on radio and in recent years on television are so obvious as to need no elaboration. There is always the threat of offending the sponsor, or the friends of the sponsor, or the Catholic people who can readily be prompted into writing the sponsor or the transmitting station.

This was brought out forcibly and to the ultimate embarrassment of the Roman hierarchy when it successfully prevented the showing of "Martin Luther" over Chicago's

WGN-TV in December of 1956. Catholic pressure in the form of letters and phone calls from deliberately agitated Catholics was successful in scaring the television station into the statement that the film revealed a "dark well of hatred" in the religious field, which could be covered only by banning the film. The counter-protests of a finally awakened Protestant citizenry resulted in the showing over another station.

An interesting point in the Roman Catholic position towards "Martin Luther" is the classification of the film by the Legion of Decency. It is *not* condemned. It has been classified alone under a new category "Unacceptable to Catholics." It is unacceptable, of course, because its truth hurts so much. In spite of the Catholic press's frantic contentions that the picture distorts the Church of the sixteenth century, every discerning priest and ex-priest knows that "Martin Luther" is meticulously accurate, even to the sloppy manner in which the monks make the sign of the cross. The picture of the German collecting relics till he had a million or more years' release from purgatory is, of course, ridiculous and places both the veneration of relics and the belief in purgatory in a ludicrous light. But hoarding of "spiritual treasures" by the medieval Catholics is historically true. Every priest should remember the story of the prince who claimed to have some of the clay that Adam was made of, a feather from the wing of the Angel Gabriel and some milk from the breast of the Virgin Mary.

The most important channel for Catholic censorship and propaganda is still the press. The hierarchy does its best to keep unfavorable news out of daily papers and our national magazines. This would include un-American activities of the clergy in other parts of the world, negotiations of the Vatican with totalitarian powers, questionable actions of the American clergy, such as the arrest of a priest for drunk and reckless driving (especially with a parishioner's wife in the same car). This censorship is usually successfully achieved through Catholic members of the newspapers' local staffs and the ever present Damocles' sword of the threat of a subscription boycott on the part of the "large" Catholic public or an advertising boycott by the Catholic merchants.

When we were in the seminary, we were not permitted to see the secular daily press at all. It was not to be trusted. We could read the nation's only Catholic daily, an anemic, newsless sheet published in Iowa, and the Catholic weeklies.

The strength of the Catholic press lies in these diocesan and national weeklies, whose combined circulation in America runs into the millions. It is a "kept" press, subserviently docile, enthusiastically and recklessly loyal, regardless of truth, and as completely under the thumb of the hierarchy and the Vatican as IZVESTIA is under the thumb of the Kremlin.

This press is the club which the bishops as a group swing over the Congress and the President of the United States, constantly insinuating the protective or primitive strength of the votes of an alleged forty million people. Judging by the way both houses of Congress and President Eisenhower unanimously jumped rabbit-like through the hoop at the close of the 1956 session and gave the Pope almost a million dollars to repair his summer palace, one would think that even Catholic children could vote.

This press successfully used this same illusion of power in intimidating state governors and their legislatures. The classic example of this tyranny over our "free" institutions has been the continual defeat of repeatedly-introduced laws to repeal the archaic and cruel birth control laws in some New England states. If the legislators of those states even remotely resembled the Catholics whose confessions I heard for many years, they were themselves practicing birth control while obediently voting against its dissemination by the doctors of their states.

This identical scare technique is used in many parts of the United States in controlling counties, cities and school districts.

The Catholic press will lie as smoothly and as volubly as the Communist or the late Fascist press to protect the Roman Church.

It pits the children of parochial schools and their parents against non-Catholics. It does so by labeling those who in any way criticize those schools or the hierarchy, no matter how justly, as bigots, anti-Catholics, and (while McCarthy was the beacon for most of the clergy) as Communist sympathizers. Bishop G. Bromley Oxnam is called "intolerant" and a friend of Communists. Dr. Joseph M. Dawson is a "bigot." These two truly Christian gentlemen and fine Americans have become the target of Roman Catholic ecclesiastical wrath by helping to found Protestants and Other Americans United, a national group dedicated to the one sole purpose of preserving the first amendment to the Constitution of the United States—separation of church and state—particularly in the schools of the country.

An outstanding classic example of vicious vituperation of Catholic "journalism" and "untouchable-ism" is the 160-page booklet, "Who's Who in the P.O.A.U.," published by the Catholic weekly, *Our Sunday Visitor*, Huntington, Indiana, March 28, 1951. Whole chapters are devoted to Protestant leaders such as Bishop Oxnam; Dr. Dawson; Dr. Poteat, the Southern Baptist; Dr. John Mackay, President of the Princeton Theological Seminary; and Paul Blanshard. Of them, the anonymous Catholic writer states in his introduction:

This book has to do with the officers and some co-workers of Protestants and Other Americans United for the Separation of Church and State. What the writer has to say about them is well documented and you will note that most of them had a pronounced pink past record. Only recently, when it is unpopular to express sympathy for Communism directly, are they helping the cause in another way.

These men are giving great encouragement to Stalin by dividing our citizenry and by their political activity against the only Church that has been arrayed against Bolshevism from the time it was born in 1918. They imitate the Maliks and Vishinskys in denouncing others but are themselves guilty of the charges they make.

With this type of journalism, Roman Catholics are, of course, deceiving only themselves and especially parochial school children. The well known Catholic author and critic, Thomas Sugrue, condemns this Catholic self-hypnosis in his book, *A Catholic Speaks His Mind*.

When in the sixteenth century, Protestantism split the Western Church in two, self-criticism vanished from the parent body, the Roman Catholic Church. Four hundred years later, in the latter half of the twentieth century, it is still absent, and

the damage its exile has caused within the Church is incalculable, incalculable because there is no way to more than hazard
what Catholicism might be today had her rulers not theorized
that criticism by Protestantism from without—a criticism expressed continuously and powerfully by the simple fact of
Protestantism's existence—made criticism from within too
dangerous to tolerate. . . .

Among those Catholics who dominate the American Church,
for example, the things I have said about their kind of Catholicism in the following pages will be denounced as anti-
Catholic, when in fact the most cursory examination of these
statements will reveal to anyone that they are instead pro-
Christian, being based on an affirmation of the metaphysics
of the Sermon on the Mount. Thus, if they are indeed anti-
Catholic, Catholicism is anti-Christian. Such Catholics as
recognize this paradox will wish, of course, to avoid its im-
plication, but they will not agree with me in my conclusions.
They will say, with the hurt look of an abandoned fawn, "Why
didn't you let somebody else say that? Aren't there enough
Protestants pouring criticism on the Church without one of
our own adding to it? We's not perfect but we're better than
they are, and anyhow, the least we can do is stick together."

My answer to this is that what I have now said is the first
thing in my life I wanted to say, and that it has burned in me
steadily since I initially felt its sting in my brain and in my
heart.

In America the Church has been used as a vehicle for the
social, economic and political ambitions of certain immigrant
groups from Europe—Italian, Irish, German, Spanish, French
—bent on building themselves from identification as poor
foreigners to recognition as middle-class Americans. It is a
natural ambition and in no way reprehensible, but it has
nothing to do with the purpose of the Church, which is to
give sustenance to her faithful in the world of the spirit and
to guide them through the labyrinths of the mind and flesh
toward God. What has happened because of this unholy alli-
ance of the Church and American free enterprise is bad for
the Church and the American Catholics involved in it.

Catholic parochial school pupils and their elders are kept in ignorance of papal political intrigue and papal power and financial graspings throughout the world. Sound books have been written on this subject. A few are those of Paul Blanshard, Avro Manhattan and John McKnight. The respectable Episcopalian magazine, *The Churchman*, (May 1, 1955; June, 1955; July, 1955) named dates and people to show the Vatican's desire for a fascistic victory in World War II, its attempts to secure ridiculous leniency for German war criminals, and its instigation and perpetuation of the "Cold War."

To any student of contemporary or past history, it is obvious that the Catholic press lies in its attempts to cloud the minds of its people.

One of the most flagrant examples of self-deception in the Catholic press concerns its treatment and evaluation of today's persecution of Protestants in Colombia, South America. Not only have most Protestant magazines carried the stories but the American press wires and weekly news magazines have supplied details of the murders of fifty-three ministers and communicants, the destruction of forty-three churches and the closing of one hundred and sixty Protestant day schools.

Colombia sorely needed those schools. Forty-five per cent of the adult population can neither read nor write. The *New Age* of August, 1955, points out that, under Colombia's Catholic government, only twelve per cent ever advance to the fourth grade and less than thirty per cent of all teachers have normal school certificates. Everybody in America knows that a vicious Roman Catholic persecution is in full swing, except American Roman Catholics. The Catholic press continues to repeat that the Protestants are lying, that no violence has taken place or, as the Catholic *Messenger* of East St. Louis stated on June 18, 1954, "charges that Protestants are being persecuted in Colombia are inaccurate or grossly exaggerated." Another Catholic paper called the whole matter a "myth." The Arizona (Catholic) REGISTER philosophized on August 28, 1954, "(Protestant) mission agencies are responsible for these stories, which bring in money."

The National Association of Evangelicals lists the names of priests who led the mobs, the dates, and places of assaults, and detailed descriptions of the destruction of property. *Time* Magazine (February 8, 1954) confirmed the persecution. But the Catholic REGISTER (February 5, 1954) laid the whole matter to rest to the satisfaction of devout Catholics, especially the parochial school children, with the simple statement "allegations that Protestants have suffered loss of life and property in its country were declared false by the Colombia government."

This technique is characteristic of the Catholic press. If unfavorable criticism should slip through the guard and be published, the usual technique of the hierarchy is not to analyze and answer the allegations but simply to condemn the critic and try to destroy his reputation and veracity. This approach of "refutation by denunciation" is very common in the Catholic press. When Paul Blanshard wrote *The Irish and Catholic Power*, the Catholic REGISTER chain screamed "Secular Fanatic Thinks Spiritual View of Life Perilous" (REGISTER, December 4, 1953) and produced nothing to prove that Blanshard was either a secularist or a fanatic. The Jesuit magazine *America* in reviewing my book, *People's*

Padre, summarized all criticism into the bold statement: "Deliberate misrepresentation, abuse of confidence, half-truths, suppression of fact, misuse of statistics and unjustified coupling of unrelated material are constant throughout the book." (*America,* May 1, 1954.)

This disregard of facts is ordered by the Pope himself. In instructions to the 1957 meeting of the Catholic Press Association (Arizona REGISTER, May 24, 1957) Pius XII informed the delegates:

... they must reflect in what they write the unity, the oneness of the Church in her faith and moral teaching. It was to His apostles and through them to their successors that Christ Our Lord confided the truth He came on earth to impart to men. Hence the teaching office in His Church, as all know, belongs to the Bishop of Rome, His Vicar on earth, for the entire body of the faithful, and to the several Bishops for the group of members of the Church confided by that Vicar to their pastoral charge.

But in carrying out their grave obligation of teaching, the Bishops will enlist the help of priests and also of the laity, whose warrant for teaching, however, will always derive not from their personal eminence in learning, but from their mission entrusted to them by the Bishops. To them the press, as all the faithful, will give loyal obedience.

The Catholic weeklies assume that their readers are historically ignorant or they would not so grossly misinform them. The following is from THE SOUTHERN CROSS, June 20, 1957, the San Diego, California, diocesan paper. One should keep in mind the four-hundred-year Holy Inquisition while reading it:

The Church established by Christ must teach His truth to all men. This is one of her chief obligations.

And in the discharge of it, she does not interfere with the free exercise of human rights; she does not coerce; she does not proselytize.

Indeed, through the ages she has been a champion of religious freedom. Her sons and daughters have promoted it here and elsewhere; they have fought for it, suffered for it and even died for it.

Yet from time to time and even today she is labeled an enemy of religious liberty. Despite her record, she is charged with aggression against other churches, even with open war against them and with insidious attempts, especially through her system of education, to overthrow the religion or religions of others.

. . . In our own country, Methodist Bishop G. Bromley Oxnam, who spews his poison perennially against the Church, now charges that the students of Georgetown University are hampered in their "pursuit of truth" and "religious liberty, together with the basic civil liberties of the Democratic order."

Another example of "news" which might raise the eyebrows of Americans paying taxes for foreign aid was the headline of the national chain of Catholic REGISTERS of June 7, 1957: JAPAN THANKS PIUS XII FOR AIDING IN RECOVERY.

Vatican City.—Japan's rise from defeat after World War II is credited largely to the efforts of the Holy See and Pius XII in a note to the Pope from Senjin Tsuruoka, Japan's Minister to the Holy See. The note thanks the Holy Father, on behalf of the Japanese government, for his efforts toward promoting that nation's welfare.

Japan will never forget all the Pope did to secure the release of Japanese prisoners after World War II. . . .

"The Japanese government and people," read the note, "respectfully appreciate the untiring efforts Your Holiness has made for many years for the peace and welfare of the whole world."

Mr. Tsuruoka stressed the fact that, when he was in charge of Japan's social security system, he had the opportunity of observing the immense benefits given the Japanese people by Catholic enterprises, which had earned the admiration of his people.

Probably the greatest lie of the Roman Catholic press is the elaborate annual reporting of Catholic statistics regarding the Church's growth, as presented by the *Official Catholic Directory* published by P. J. Kennedy & Sons of New York.

The Arizona REGISTER, May 24, 1957, figures showed 34,563,851 Roman Catholics in America. The figure used in 1960 is 40,000,000. This is enough to make every Catholic proud of his faith and enough to scare every politician in the nation. That is exactly the result the hierarchy wishes to achieve by publishing the figures.

An analysis of how these statistics are compiled will show how unreliable they are. In the first place no one is ever dropped from Catholic figures. As one priest wrote about me: ". . . there are no ex-Catholics, there are merely bad Catholics." Furthermore, contrary to the custom of most Protestant churches, all baptized babies are considered as part of the Catholic populace.

These accounting procedures are, however, not the important aspect of the utter falseness of Catholic statistics and therefore of Catholic political strength.

The truth is that Catholics in the United States are, in most dioceses, not counted at all. The pattern of the compilation of Roman Catholic statistics should interest Protestants who are so precise in their membership rolls.

There are, as such, no membership rolls in Catholic churches. Some parishes have a census of sorts, some have lists of regular contributors. But practically no Catholic pastor of a large parish in America knows how many good, bad or indifferent Catholics live within the geographical boundaries of his parish.

This is, in the first place, due to the fact that, when Roman Catholics move from one parish to another or from one city to another, there is no constituted machinery in Catholicism to keep track of them. There are no letters of transfer or "demit" so common in Protestant organizations.

All a Catholic has to do when he moves to a new area is to go to Mass on Sunday—anywhere. Nor is it customary in Catholic churches to ask newcomers or visitors to rise or to fill out a card that might be used for statistical control. Only when there is a baptism, a wedding or a funeral to be performed need a Catholic identify himself to any priest. Barring these functions, a Catholic might well attend a large Catholic church for half a century without the clergy knowing that he is there or who he is.

The annual publication of the Roman Catholic "strength" in America is for several purposes. One is so that the hierarchy of America can scare the politicians and businessmen of the nation. Another is so that the Roman pastors can impress their bishops and the bishops can impress the Pope. The success of all these clerics is based largely on the numerical growth of the faithful under their care, not on their fidelity or their devotion to the Church.

The average pastor of a Catholic church is as removable from his "job" at the whim of his bishop as was the medieval knave or jester at the whim of the king. His parish has nothing to say as to his tenure of office. There are "irremovable" pastors; but I can recall from theological seminary days the discussions on the "twenty-one ways of removing an irremovable pastor."

The life of an average American Roman Catholic pastor is a comfortable one. It is positively lush in the larger parishes of the big cities. No pastor wants to return to the sometimes cruel servitude of being an "assistant" or the penury and lack of a future in pastoring the small country parishes, which usually serve as the disciplinary "Siberias" for every bishop. I can remember a priest condemned to Willcox, Arizona, who told me that he was able to physically survive only by mass offerings from his out-of-state friends and by watching from his parsonage window the slot machine in the bus station cafe. He had studied the percentages and, when enough bus patrons had warmed up the "bandit," he would slip over from his sacristy and play until he cashed in on the jackpot.

The pastor is caught on the horns of a dilemma. His annual contribution to the support of the bishops, the *cathedraticum,* is based on the numerical membership of his parish. Therefore, to save money, he should keep that figure low. On the other hand his retention of his pastorate, with its financial and other emoluments, depends on his showing enough progress in numbers so that his bishop will not be embarrassed at the annual meeting of the American hierarchy or particularly on the occasion of his regular *Ad Limina* (to the threshold) visits to the Pope in Rome.

From this dilemma has evolved a pattern. Almost every pastor in the United States checking his carbon of the previous year's report shows a gain in numbers. This protects his job. He makes that gain as small as he can get by with. This protects his church's bankbook—over which he is the sole custodian and which he can save or squander at his own discretion. There are no financial lay trustees in Catholic churches.

And so almost every pastor in the United States shows a gain in the number of Catholics when he sends his annual report back to P. J. Kennedy & Sons of New York, through his local chancery office. Usually the only pastors who refuse to pad their figures are the older priests who went to school with the bishop and perhaps know where some of the episcopal bodies are buried.

The reported increase in the number of American Catholics in the ten years from 1947 to 1957 was 9,295,678 (Arizona REGISTER, May 24, 1957) or almost one million per year. According to the 1957 *Official Catholic Directory*, the 1956 increase was 989,834. The figure looks impressive—at first glance. The same report, however, boasts of the total of 16,345 parishes in America. This means an increase of only sixty people per parish per year, or about one person per week—and *this includes newborn* babies.

The average Southern Baptist preacher would relinquish his pulpit and go back to farming, fishing or to the factory if he couldn't do better than that.

One interesting aspect in the operation of our hospital also shows how meaningless are the glowing figures of the Catholic press. In our Memorial Hospital we keep an accurate check on the religious affiliations of our patients. The following figures have run consistently true for several years. In spite of the opposition of the local clergy, we average about three thousand Roman Catholics per year. Every new admission is asked if he will permit his clergyman to visit him. Only ten per cent of these self-proclaimed Catholics will permit a priest to see them. Ninety per cent refuse to see a priest. Only three per year, or .001 per cent, ask for a priest.

The Catholic press might tone down its boasting, if it realized how weak is its control over its own people. Our Protestants and politicians might take heart enough to be real Americans if they could only realize that the Catholic press in America is nothing but "sounding brass or a tinkling cymbal" and that Roman Catholic loyalty in America is confined to an unthinking minority and its alleged strength is purely a myth. The great strength of the Catholic hierarchy rests only in the fear of Protestant ministers with their boards and the fear of merchants who shrink from losing a Catholic dollar.

In *People's Padre* I told of Catholic attempts to "censor" me personally—by spreading false rumors as to my health or my morals; by condemning me in the Catholic press, by attempting to discredit me at our hospital, by trying to discredit the hospital when that failed and even by trying to kill me.

Since the *People's Padre* was published, these efforts have taken every form of censorship and boycott.

The Beacon Press itself tells the story of the silent treatment:

On April 7, 1954, *People's Padre* was published. It was received with silence. Eighteen months after publication, the files show that in New England and Middle Atlantic states only two newspaper reviews had appeared. These were in the *Worcester Telegram* and *Afro-American*, where Saunders Redding reported that he had read *People's Padre* "with unquiet but deep satisfaction." One New York paper, in a round-up of books, referred to Mr. McLoughlin's book as "apt to be . . . highly controversial." *The American Library Association Booklist* reported it was "an interesting document, but unacceptable to Catholic readers," and the *Library Journal* said: "Libraries should buy with caution." Caution proved to be the watchword: One distinguished paper more than a year ago asked the noted theologian Reinhold Niebuhr to review *People's Padre.* He prepared the review but the paper has not published it.

In a *Christianity and Crisis* editorial, Mr. Niebuhr wrote: "*People's Padre* deserves attention on two counts. It deserves attention because of its intrinsic merits. . . . The second reason for commending the volume is that the journals of America have paid practically no attention to it. The publishers, The Beacon Press, state that it has been systematically ignored by newspapers. One wonders whether explicit Catholic pressure or merely fear of Catholic reprisals has made American publishers so craven. In any case, the incident illustrates one of the dangers to our democratic freedoms . . ."

One of the three major women's magazines asked the Beacon Press for a review copy of *People's Padre.* The editor had thought of serializing the story. He returned it with the statement that "although we are not cowards neither do we want to commit suicide."

A west coast editor of *Collier's* visited me to gather preliminary material for a story on my break with the Catholic priesthood. He was pessimistic about the possibility of the story's publication because of *Collier's* fear of Roman Catholic reprisals. The current technique of the hierarchy, he said, was not even to contact the magazine itself but rather to approach the national firms advertising in the magazine and to threaten them with a boycott of thirty million customers at that time, if they continued to "support anti-Catholic" publications.

Many disillusioned Catholics, especially high school students, have told me that, when they asked the clergy if they might read my book or asked for a refutation of it after they had dared to read it, the priests made no attempt to prove me wrong. They merely stated that I was insane, a liar, a drunkard, that God had cursed me, that I was paralyzed, that I was turning to stone, that I had muscular dystrophy, that I had divorced my wife— and, as a result, that I was completely unreliable.

When the book first appeared, a priest, claiming to represent all the clergy of Arizona, called the manager of Arizona's largest bookstore, Martindale's in Phoenix, and ordered him to take the copies out of the windows and off the counters. He said that, if the store did not discontinue the sale of the book, all Catholics would be asked to boycott the store. When the first display was placed in the Horner-Payne Book Store of Phoenix, catsup was smeared over the windows. Several frantic Catholics had the nerve and bad taste even to call the Phoenix Baptist Book Store and curse its lady manager.

During the years since the book's release, a very large number of people have written to me for the name of the publisher; because book stores were intimidated. The writers who became interested in "detective" games elected to watch the book stores in major cities and to routinely request the book. Many stores, they said, carried the book under the counter, others offered to get it— "this is a Catholic city, you know, and we don't dare display a book that might offend them."

One remarkable phenomenon that came home to me

during this book's career is how easily a community can become a "Catholic city." I have had it in letters from New York, Chicago, Boston (of course), Washington, D. C., Des Moines, Dubuque, Albuquerque, San Francisco, Denver, Seattle and many, many others.

During the Billy Graham crusade in New York City in 1957 it was repeatedly stated in the papers that the city was only twenty-seven per cent Roman Catholic. All that was necessary to establish a "Catholic city" was for a handful of Catholics, frequently school children, with a nun along, to enter a book store and threaten the book store with the boycott of the "vast numbers" of Catholics in the city. Of course, the boycott generally doesn't happen and, if so, doesn't do any harm.

When Martindale's in Phoenix was blacklisted, the manager doubled the number of *People's Padre* in the street windows and interspersed them with Bishop Sheen's book. He told me that, in his experience, a Catholic book blacklisting always failed. He said that the reason is that there are so few literate devout Catholics who pay any attention to the fulminations of the clergy that their loss can't even be felt by a book store. His store has sold more than five thousand copies of *People's Padre*.

He and his clerks have delighted in telling me through the years of priests and nuns coming into the store and, when they recognized no Catholic patrons, slyly picking up the book and paying for it nervously; as though they had just bought a year's supply of the worst pornographic literature. A clerk in the book store of the Kansas City railroad station told me she enjoyed watching nuns passing through the city (feeling they were unknown) quickly buying the book and slipping it into the voluminous folds of their robes.

Our hospital gift shop has sold thousands of copies of the book. One morning a doctor waved a copy before me, "Sister Mary ———— at St. Joseph's Hospital asked me to buy this for her but to keep it quiet. She says she has to read it to be able to refute it."

This letter is from a Catholic college teacher in California whose family lives in Phoenix:

In addition to saying "thank you," I thought it might amuse you to learn of the travels of one copy of your book, *People's Padre.*

When it was first published, Mike, of course, bought a copy. I asked him to send it to me after he and my mother had finished reading it. (I couldn't possibly afford to buy my own copy, being a public school teacher.) He agreed to my request and I waited for the book to arrive.

And I waited—and I waited. Finally in a letter I asked when they were going to send it, thinking they had forgotten. I received an answer to the letter, but no mention was made of your book. The next time I was in Phoenix I asked them point blank why they hadn't sent it. Mike, rather shamefacedly, admitted that he had loaned it to a friend. Pete, the friend, after reading it had loaned it to a friend of his and on and on. But Mike assured me that he would get it back and send it very soon.

Months passed. Still no book. During Christmas holidays this year I gave Mike a bad time again, and we went through the routine. One day while I was there, friend Pete dropped in at the house so I decided to start solving the difficulty by approaching him.

After a few minutes of polite badinage, Pete finally admitted that several months back and somewhere along the way, one of the friends had a sick friend. This sick friend was in St. Joseph's, so friend of sick friend decided to take him your book. As far as Pete knew the book was still circulating through St. Joseph's, surreptitiously, of course, but enjoying great popularity. Before leaving, Pete solemnly promised to go up to St. Joseph's himself and retrieve it. I assume that he fulfilled his promise because Saturday I received it in the mail.

Unfortunately, I have no sick friends in Catholic hospitals, so cannot continue to spread your word in that manner. I can, however, loan it to the interested and literate faculty here. They will not be as appropriate a reading audience as the group as St. Joseph's, but this should accomplish one end: that of diverting their coffee time discussions from the relative merits and demerits of California Retirement System B to the relative merits and demerits of Emmett McLoughlin.

You may stop reading at this point. What follows is the capsule criticism that most readers feel qualified or rash enough to give.

As a personal mental catharsis it is easy to recognize its value. From the standpoint of acquainting, and attempting to arouse, Catholics from their complacent mental lethargy in regard to the hierarchy and dictates of the church it is a definite and worthwhile contribution. It is in regard to this aspect that I would like to express a thought, possibly a stimulus.

Although a future publication along these lines may be of doubtful commercial value, it appears that a more detailed discussion of many concepts would be beneficial. Your citing of sections from "Moral Theology" and subsequent comments were of definite interest. Your quotes from Canon Law, and from the Syllabus of Errors, present excellent factual material. Apparently, you are one of the few people in a position to make a legitimate contribution to a discussion of the relationship of modern life to Catholicism.

Perhaps this whole discussion could have been condensed by stating: "You did well—now why don't you do more?"

The pattern of Roman Catholic censorship is, of course, to prevent the faithful from learning any truth that may be unfavorable to it or may excite disturbing thoughts or doubts among them. Any critical book, including *People's Padre* or this one, falls into this character and, if possible, must either be suppressed or discredited; or Catholics must be kept away from it.

Worse than the travails of being a controversial author are those of being a controversial lecturer—especially on the subject of the Catholic Church—especially when that lecturer is a former priest.

My introduction to the physical dangers of lecturing in a free democracy on the Catholic religion occurred in Phoenix. I had been giving a series of talks on Catholicism in Southern Baptist churches. When leaving a church one night, I noticed a friend—a deputy sheriff and his squad car. He was also an ex-Catholic and had left the Church at the same time that I did. I jokingly asked him if he was trying to "get religion" in his old age. He told me that, because of reports of threats on my life, there had been at least two armed deputies at each of my talks and there would continue to be.

Of course, physical violence is not recommended by the Catholic clergy when ex-priests speak, but it is frequently threatened or implied.

When I finished speaking at the annual meeting of Protestants and Other Americans United in Constitution Hall, Washington, D. C., in January of 1954, I was surrounded by a solemn-faced group of husky young men who looked like some gangster goon squad or a basketball team. I tipped off the Master of Ceremonies that trouble was coming up. He sent word out for reinforcements. I asked the boys what Catholic school they attended. They said "Georgetown University" and informed me that most of them were studying for the Jesuit priesthood. Their spokesman said they could not permit me to give such speeches. I asked him to quote a mis-statement. "That makes no difference," he said, "what you said hurts our Church and we cannot permit that." A discerning janitor turned off the lights and my wife and I got off the platform.

On another occasion, while I was speaking in a Washington, D. C., church, Catholic hecklers phoned during the service, said the church would be dynamited if my address was not stopped.

In Brockton, Massachusetts, November 5, 1956, while I was speaking in a Congregational Church, the floodlights were smashed in front of the church.

In the First Baptist Church in Santa Monica, California, Catholics were planted in anterooms. They stopped me as I went by and repeated the obviously rehearsed message: "Father, we are Catholics and we're here to pray for you. Don't despair. You'll come back."

In Long Beach, California, on this same tour, a "converted ex-priest" jumped up in the middle of my lecture in an effort to embarrass me and try to stop the program.

In Albuquerque, New Mexico, among a sprinkling of hecklers, was one who asked me to confess if I were really happy. When I emphatically stated that I was, she turned to the person next to her and stated in a loud voice, "He's not happy. He just thinks he is!"

In Worcester, Massachusetts, in November, 1956, the Council of Churches was afraid to sponsor me because of Catholic reprisals both on the churches and, through their businesses, on the various deacons and church board members. An individual decided to handle the program.

He applied for the use of Worcester's Municipal Auditorium. Its board (four of the six were Roman Catholics) rejected the application on the grounds that I was a controversial figure and would disturb the religious harmony of the city. This "harmony" exists because Roman Catholics are in complete control. My friend rented the venerable Mechanics' Hall from its private owners. He went then to the Chief of Police to buy protection. The Chief was unable to furnish four Protestant policemen to guarantee harmony. On the brighter side, it was necessary to hold two meetings; and dozens of Catholic priests were scattered through both audiences.

In Des Moines, Iowa, I spoke in a Methodist Church. Just before the meeting the pastor slipped back into his office and told me and the other ministers that twelve Catholic priests in their Roman collars were in the front row. It was obviously an intimidating show of force by a group who would normally no more enter a Methodist church than they would accept an injection of bubonic plague. I told the minister that their presence would not bother me; in fact, I would enjoy giving them a few disturbing thoughts that would give them bad dreams for a long time.

"But," I added, "they may be loaded to cause us trouble in the question and answer period." He felt assured that he could handle that. That night I stressed more strongly than usual the contradiction between American freedom of thought, of speech and worship and the refusal of those freedoms to Catholics. The presiding pastor stopped any subsequent oration from any of the priests by offering his pulpit to them the following Sunday morning, providing they would extend him the same courtesy. At the end of the program he went down and greeted each priest personally. One of them said, "I could have refuted every argument that ex-priest gave but, before we came in, the Monsignor here, our Superior, forbade any of us to say anything."

In Springfield, Missouri, I spoke in the spring of 1957 to a city-wide Protestant rally, sparked by the Methodists, but held in the First Baptist Church. The Sunday afternoon program was broadcast by both radio and television. When it was over, the pastor came to me and enthusiastically told me that I had united all the Protestants of southwestern Missouri.

I asked, "How come?"

"During your speech the phone kept ringing. All callers were Catholics denouncing me for having you. One threatened to kill me before the week is out. You know what threats like that will do to the backbone of a Southern Baptist preacher."

The theme that had aroused the Catholics (I received nasty letters for a couple of weeks) was: "The Importance and Function of a Protestant Hospital in a Protestant Community."

All of these examples of un-American repression and persecution were unpleasant. I have learned, however, to expect them and to live with them and adjust to them as any thoughtful Negro must, while still struggling for the full warmth and richness of democracy, still reconcile himself to the hard facts of life and know that the "fullness of the Gospel" is still a "fur piece" away.

In the spring of 1957, the Hockenbury System of Harrisburg, Pennsylvania, conducted a drive in Phoenix for the expansion of our Memorial Hospital from one hundred and eighty-nine to three hundred and fifty beds. The drive was successful but it was almost over the dead bodies of the Roman Catholics of Phoenix. Some ten years previously, the Catholic hospital of Phoenix, St. Joseph's, had solicited all individuals and firms on the premise that it was a community enterprise, designed to serve all the public impartially. It was generously supported by individuals, businesses and utilities. When it opened it operated, as do all Catholic hospitals, not in the interests of the community but under the Catholic code of medical ethics. This meant, of course, no birth control information, no matter how necessary; no abortions, no matter how necessary, even to save the life of a doomed mother.

When our drive was over and my assistants and I went over all the "reject" pledge cards, we were astounded at the bigotry of individuals and firms who, when asked to help Memorial Hospital, stated: "No, I am a Catholic." "Our firm supports only Catholic drives." "All our charity, since we are Catholics, goes to the Good Shepherd Convent." Et cetera.

The most shocking of all was the Cudahy Packing Company. It has a huge packing plant in Phoenix. For years we had purchased the bulk of our meat from it because of its convenience and the fact that it employed Phoenix people. I had known that the company was Roman Catholic—of sorts. While a student at Santa Barbara Mission, I knew, as did every other student, how our poverty-vowed superiors fawned on "Good Queen Bess," —Elizabeth Cudahy, for her financial favors. And I had heard a variety of stories about the other members of the family.

Our dietary steward and myself waited upon the manager of the local Cudahy plant with no results. Later we were informed that, since the Cudahys were such a strong Catholic family and had contributed so heavily to St. Joseph's Hospital, we could not expect any contribution.

CHAPTER EIGHT

School Beyond The State

It is commonly assumed by American citizens, both Catholic and non-Catholic, that Roman Catholic parochial schools must meet the same standards as to teacher qualifications, curriculum content, student attendance, and textbooks as the public schools of the state. This is not true.

In most states, the textbooks, subject matter and teacher qualifications of parochial schools are entirely up to the teaching nuns, the local pastor or the bishop of the diocese. If they match the local public schools, it is because of the pressure of interchange of pupils between the two systems. Or it may be because of the indirect necessity for parochial high schools to meet the requirements of state universities or to maintain membership in the North Central Association or other secondary school associations.

The Arizona State Superintendent of Public Instruction told me that the State of Arizona has absolutely no educational control over the parochial schools. The teachers do not have to meet any standards. The teaching nuns do not even have to be grammar school graduates. He can enforce no norms of curriculum, textbooks or annual days of attendance. His office has no record of the names or the number of parochial schools in the state or any attendance records. The state has a compulsory school age law; but the state must assume that all youngsters not enrolled in public schools are enrolled in parochial schools.

This educational chaos might be considered a hangover of the primitiveness of the "law West of the Pecos." Surprisingly, it obtains in most states.

Protestants and Other Americans United conducted a survey of all states in 1954 and arrived at this conclusion, according to *Church and State,* September, 1954, page 5:

Are private and parochial school pupils in the United States given a basic education "equivalent" to that given public school pupils? The results of a *Church and State* country-wide survey of state education laws and policies, published below, reveal that *in most instances public authorities do not know the answer because they exercise no effective control over the conduct of non-public schools.*

The following quotes from a few state departments of education are typical:

ARIZONA. "Our State Department of Public Instruction has no jurisdiction over private and parochial schools; therefore, we receive no records from them." "There is no requirement that they meet the standards of public schools."

CALIFORNIA. ". . . Private schools prepare their own examinations, and no information is available on comparative results as between public and private schools.

Length of the private school day need not conform to the public school day. Private school teachers are theoretically supposed to meet the same standards as public school teachers but are not required to have the same credentials."

COLORADO. "Colorado has no jurisdiction over any private or parochial schools and has established no minimum standards for such schools."

FLORIDA. "The State Department of Education . . . has no authority over the parochial schools. . . . Schools are asked to report their attendance through the county superintendents to this office, most of which is not done."

IDAHO. An official wrote: "The state has no regulatory powers over private or parochial schools."

INDIANA. An official wrote: "The State requests registration of teachers and teaching qualifications—the parochial schools seldom cooperate in this matter. No action is taken if the request is ignored. . . . The city and county superintendents are free to visit these schools but very seldom do . . . nor are (such schools) required to make annual reports for the Department of Public Instruction files. . . ."

KENTUCKY. "In this state, teachers in private schools are not required to have certificates, but in practice most of them do."

LOUISIANA. A state official wrote: ". . . children who attend unapproved schools are considered as being in compliance with the Compulsory Education Law. . . . Private schools are free to seek state approval or to do without it, as they choose. . . . There is no state policy for the periodic inspection of private schools by state officials."

MINNESOTA. "Certification of non-public school teachers is voluntary. The state does not prepare minimum standards for non-public schools, nor does it inspect them."

NEW JERSEY. ". . . Any private school controlled or operated by a charitable institution . . . by a religious denomination" is exempt from the law providing state supervision of private schools.

NEW YORK. "Non-public instruction 'shall be at least substantially equivalent' to public school instruction in the 'ten common school branches' of learning, and for at least one hundred and ninety days a year. A school operated by 'an established religious group' is not required to register under state regulations."

OKLAHOMA. "Under Oklahoma laws this Department has nothing to do with private schools so far as licensing is concerned."

PENNSYLVANIA. Schools "owned and operated by bona fide religious institutions" are exempt from licensing requirements affecting academic schools which accept tuition. Certain courses, flag observances, medical examinations, vaccinations, and the like, are required of all schools, but standard state examinations in required courses are not provided.

SOUTH CAROLINA. "We have practically no laws of a regulatory nature applicable to private schools."

SOUTH DAKOTA. "School accreditation is not required, and standard examinations are not provided."

TENNESSEE. "In Tennessee we do not have any State Standards that apply to private schools. . . . By this statement we simply mean that if some of our Tennessee children are enrolled in private or parochial schools and they are not seen loafing about in public places, it is assumed that they are meeting the attendance requirements. . . ."

UTAH. "Utah has no laws regarding standards for private schools. All that is necessary . . . to establish a private school is to take out a license."

VERMONT. Non-public school teachers need not be certified, and non-public elementary schools need not make reports. Inspection visits are not made.

WASHINGTON. "State law does not require the licensing and inspection of private schools. . . . Reports are legally required from non-public schools, but since there is no supervision by public school authorities, and particularly because there is no penalty provided for failure to file such reports, the reporting is not complete."

WEST VIRGINIA. An official expressed his "regret that we do not have any definite information or, for that matter, full information concerning private and parochial schools. . . ."

WYOMING. "There is no provision for the certification of teachers of non-public schools and this office has no jurisdiction over such schools."

CHAPTER NINE

Critics Speak from Many Vantages

Earlier I gave my personal opinion of the education I had received in the school system of the Roman Catholic Church. What follows constitutes the opinions of others, principally of Catholic critics regarding the intellectual aspects of Catholic education.

The famous Father Edward McGlynn wrote:

"It is a notorious fact which will be cheerfully acknowledged by hundreds of priests who are compelled in spite of themselves to get up parochial schools, that the teaching in the parochial schools is altogether inferior to that of the public."[1]

That giant oak of American Catholicism, Cardinal Gibbons, wrote to Pope Leo XIII, December 30, 1890, that difficulties and divisions between Catholics and Protestants in America "are caused above all by the opposition against the system of national education which is attributed to us, and which, more than any other thing creates and maintains in the minds of the American people the conviction that the Catholic Church is opposed by principle to the institutions of the country and that a sincere Catholic cannot be a loyal citizen of the United States."[2]

A generation later the *Atlantic Monthly* (February, 1928) printed the mental unburdening of an anonymous priest under the title, "The Heresy of the Parochial School."

"We are a people self-ostracized. Our children may not sit in the same classroom with the child of the unorthodox. We must have our own schools, our own charities, our own graveyards. . . . When the Catholic child is six years old, he is taken to an inquisition as relentless as that over which presided the notorious Torquemada.

"More damage is done to tender souls by the intellectual lack of the parochial schoolroom than was done to the bodies of other victims of the past." . . .

The anonymous priest cited a formidable bill of particulars:

"Its fault is that it fails to develop the intellect which it crams. It makes parrot-like Christians. It trains the youth in stereotyped arguments. It stunts the religious growth of its victims.

"Not only are the minds of the children over-burdened with religious teaching, but their eyes are surfeited with pietistic teachings. Holy pictures and statues are kept constantly before them. Hour after hour they must gaze morbidly on the bleeding figure of an agonized Christ on the Cross. The same monotonous strain is pressed into their ears. They must listen to doggerel hymns, filled with sentimental piety. Their readers are composed of pious stories, too, which they hear over and over again."

In our day, too, a few voices cry out in the wilderness of Roman Catholic complacency.

Joseph E. Cunneen, a Catholic, under the heading "Catholics and Education," says: "Many Catholics today are privately asking themselves if our present attempt in education is yielding a maximum return from the effort expended."[3]

"It is extremely unfortunate that we Catholic parents have, in the main, been encouraged to be passive—paying, but non-voting—members in a school system that is usually justified as a defense of our rights. . . . When the quality of graduates is criticized, it soon becomes clear that the inadequacy of our schools is both part cause and part reflection of the level of American Catholicism in general. The process of religious erosion is going on, not only in some mechanistically oriented public school classes in biology; it is present in even more frightening form in the collective yawn at the mass attended by the entire student body of a Catholic school."[4]

In the field of science, other Catholic students may have fared better than I did in St. Anthony's Seminary —but not much better. From Notre Dame University come these words of Julian Pleasants, one of its research scientists. He was writing on the subject, "Catholics and Scientists." Again, the year is 1954:

The modern American Catholic apparently places a very low value on creative activity. Scientific research is just one of these activities. Literature and art are others. Even in the field of creative social reform where Christian motivation might be expected to be singularly effective, it is hard to escape the impression that American Catholics were moved into their present positions not by any inner sense of responsibility for inventing new social reforms, but by ulterior motives such as the fear of losing the working classes, or the fear of Communism.

(Author's note: From 1934 to 1948, while a Catholic priest, I argued fruitlessly for the opening of Catholic hospitals and universities to Negroes. After the 1954 Supreme Court decision abolishing school segregation, the United States Roman Catholic hierarchy contended that desegregation is the only Christian position and that it has been for integration all the time. It has not yet desegregated all of its own Catholic schools of nursing.)

This prevailing philosophy of the life of Catholics is almost sheer formalism, obedience to certain arbitrary prescriptions for the sake of an arbitrary reward. . . . Formalism provides no status for the virtues of science, art and prudence, since they are meaningless to someone who already has all the answers. The idea of Christian life as charity working with the tools of science, art and prudence to redeem the world becomes equally meaningless. Formalism is the peculiar temptation to which the American Catholic has for the moment succumbed. . . .

The difference in scientific accomplishment between Catholics and non-Catholics is still striking, and the simple explanations simply do not explain. The plea of Catholic poverty induced by support of a separate school system has its element of truth, yet there are other expensive educational activities that Catholic schools manage to maintain in good condition such as law schools and athletic teams. Ours is not an abject but a discriminating poverty; it lays bare our scale of values by indicating what we feel we can do without. . . .

The Catholic is willing to use the latest antibiotic and is glad that somebody took the trouble to find it. Yet he does almost nothing to help find a new antibiotic. It is not worth his trouble. . . . We even seem to be enjoying the ride. But we do not pull an oar.[5]

Mr. Pleasants' despair over Catholics in science is certainly confirmed by the *Fortune* survey of outstanding young American scientists, conducted in 1954. Not one is a Roman Catholic—among the hierarchy's claimed membership at that time of thirty-two million people.

In the field of general literature also, brave Catholics bemoan their intellectual poverty.

Frank Sheed is the co-owner of the outstanding Catholic publishing house, Sheed and Ward. In 1944, he won the Christian Culture Award. Later he became a member of the Gallery of Living Catholic Authors and in 1948 was granted the Catholic Literary Award. In 1951, the Scheil School of Social Service gave him the Pope Leo XIII medal and in 1953 he received the Cardinal Newman award. The Roman Catholic Benedictine magazine, *The Grail*, quotes Mr. Sheed in August, 1954, pages 1 and 5: "There are no first class Catholic authors under thirty-five . . . if we had a Catholic reading public, by grace of God the Catholic writers would come. . . . What we need is a reading public with a Catholic mind . . . *a grown up Catholic mind does not exist.*"

The Arizona (Catholic) REGISTER, March 11, 1955, admitted: "Catholics today number only about five per cent of the top ten thousand writers of the country. This is considered to be far short of a representative quota."

The Catholic literary critic, Henry Rago, strongly condemns the mental literary habits of his co-religionists: "There is literature and then, miserere, there is 'Catholic' literature. Literature has to be good: Catholic literature has to be 'Catholic.' It is as if one read each of these literatures with a separate sensibility; or where 'Catholic' literature is concerned, with insensibility. . . . How stubborn this habit of judgment is, I do not have to tell the conscientious teacher in the Catholic universities or the conscientious critic in the few literate Catholic magazines." [6] . . .

"The best critics in America are, most of them, not Catholic. The most pure-minded reading of literature is done, generally speaking, at the non-Catholic universities. . . . Nor can I soften these remarks by agreement with those who speak of a Catholic literary revival. I do not think it exists in America." [7]

It is important to re-emphasize that these previous quotations are not from a critical non-Catholic volume. *Catholicism in America,* from which they all come, is a Roman Catholic book.

A professor of the Department of Sociology of Notre Dame University, John J. Kane, has presented some thoughts that might explain the contradiction between the extravagant praise of the parochial school by the masses of Catholics and that system's obvious inferiority. American Catholics, he says, by inference, are so low in the intellectual and social scale that even a bad school system looks good to them—especially if their local priest says so. "In the sociological literature it appears that most Catholics fall into the middle and lower classes, perhaps more specifically into the lower middle and lower classes. This does not deny *some* membership in the upper middle class and a *sprinkling* in the classes above." [8]

Professor Kane also emphasizes that, proportionately, less than half as many Catholic youngsters go to college as Jewish—and a third less than Protestants. He shows, furthermore, "that even when Catholics obtain college degrees, they are less successful in obtaining the higher positions than Jewish and Protestant graduates." He quotes surveys to show that Catholic college graduates constitute a third of those receiving *less* than three thousand dollars per year.[9]

About half of Catholic college men become priests and lawyers. The other half are thinly spread over the professions and business and some two per cent are in the natural and social sciences.

The most startling revelation of all in Dr. Kane's study is the rating of universities on the basis of their graduates' appearance in *Who's Who in America*. His first survey (1929) listed one hundred and forty American Universities. Only two Catholic colleges appeared at all: Notre Dame ranked 137th, Xavier University 138th. In the second analysis, two hundred universities were scored. St. Louis University was first among Catholic colleges, but 139th in the over-all group. Notre Dame ranked 155th among all colleges, Georgetown 161st, Holy Cross 171st and Xavier 200th. There are two hundred and sixteen Catholic universities and colleges in America. To paraphrase the New Testament story of the healed lepers, "Where are the other" two hundred and eleven Catholic schools? Not even mentioned scholastically were Fordham, Villanova, Santa Clara, Loyola, Duquesne, Georgetown, Boston College, Creighton and the other Jesuit universities or that giant of the hierarchy, the Catholic University of America.

Dr. Kane concludes his study on a note of almost hopeless pessimism:

There may be some kind of lower middle or lower class orientation among them to education and occupation which tends to anchor Catholics in the lower socio-economic groups and which limits those who do achieve higher education to certain fields which appear to offer more security albeit less prestige and income. . . . It seems that Catholics creep forward rather than stride forward in American society and the position of American Catholics in the mid-twentieth century is better, but not so much better than it was a century ago. Neither is it as high as one might expect from such a sizable minority with a large educational system and reputed equality of opportunity in a democracy.[10]

It should be re-emphasized that Dr. Kane is a Roman Catholic in a Roman Catholic university.

Newsweek (October 10, 1955) quoted Father John Tracy Ellis, for thirteen years professor of Church History at the Catholic University of America:

"In no western society is the intellectual prestige of Catholicism lower than in the country where, in such respects as wealth, numbers and strength of organization, it is so powerful." . . . and he adds, "No well informed American Catholic will attempt to challenge that statement . . . The chief blame lies with the Catholics themselves. It lies in their frequently self-imposed ghetto mentality which prevents them from mingling as they should with their non-Catholic colleagues, and in their lack of industry and the habits of work."

It has been pointed out earlier that the Catholic school system exists principally to mould Catholics. Perhaps the most scathing condemnation of that system is by the Catholic, William Osborne, in the Catholic magazine, *Commonweal*, September 29, 1955, page 609. He contends that the Catholic school system fails even in training good Catholics.

In the realm of Catholic education, while there is evidence of a commendably ethical pattern of student behavior and an adherence to the Sacraments, there are equally disturbing indications of a Christianity that is shallow and of a lack of that spirit of detachment which partakes of the essence of spirituality and which is the antithesis of American life. The things which Catholic schools and colleges take for granted, the assumptions upon which they operate, offer a more valid insight into these deficiencies than do the eulogistic assertions in catalogues or commencement oratory. Among these assumptions is the virtue of scholastic achievements, for implicitly and explicitly our schools pay homage to scholarship. Then there is athletic prowess; in some quarters it ranks higher than in others, but numerous teachers and professors are often found in the sports parade along with their students. The school yearbook and paper, the proms with music by "name" bands and held in the luxurious settings of the better hotels—all such things speak volumes about Catholic education. . . .

A college instructor who recently queried his students on their reading habits found that *Life, Time,* The *New Yorker,* Hemingway, Greene and Waugh received most frequent mention; *Commonweal* or *America* was read with regularity by a fourth of the class. But none had read through the New Testament; only one-fifth had read a life of Christ or of any of the saints. . . .

Perhaps the most tragic aspect of our deficiencies lies in the lack of awareness of the depths, the almost exasperating depths, of Christianity. All too often, teachers of Religion seem reluctant to admit the inadequacy of their courses, probably because they feel it would be a reflection on themselves or on the particular school. What they do not realize is that the problem is something beyond their immediate control, that religious instruction is bound to suffer when it must share the curriculum with a host of more pressing and practical mundane courses, and when it must compete for student interest.

Dr. Kane's study was paralleled by the assignment of

one Chesly Manly of the Chicago TRIBUNE in 1957 to make a study to "determine the top ten American universities and the ten leaders in the co-educational men's and women's colleges—and tell why." *Newsweek*, May 6, 1957, carried the results of his survey. Not a Roman Catholic school appeared in any winning category. The top schools were:

Universities	Co-ed Colleges	Men's Colleges	Women's Colleges
1. Harvard	Oberlin	Haverford	Bryn Mawr
2. Yale	Swarthmore	Amherst	Radcliffe
3. California	Carleton	Kenyon	Barnard
4. Chicago	Reed	Wesleyan	Vassar
5. Columbia	Pomona	Hamilton	Mount Holyoke
6. Princeton	Grinnell	Union	Wellesley
7. Michigan	Lawrence	Bowdoin	Smith
8. Cornell	College of Wooster	University of the South	Goucher
9. Wisconsin	Kalamazoo	Washington and Lee	Pembroke
10. Stanford	Hope	Williams	Randolph-Macon

Manly stated that, when his studies were announced, half of those who phoned or wrote in objection were Roman Catholics; because none of their schools made the grade at all.

For the past several years, as I have lectured across the country, I have conducted an informal survey among public school teachers in high schools and colleges as to the relative preparation and ability of parochial school graduates and those of public schools.

My questionnaire was directed principally to high school teachers in smaller communities where there are Catholic grammar schools, but not Catholic high schools. It seemed that the teachers could thus compare the parochial school and the public school product quite objectively.

The following questions were based on my own experiences and the advice of public school teachers. The percentage answers of the teachers are given:

1. Which seem better prepared to pursue high school courses?

Parochial school children	10%
Public school children	90%

2. In the following studies and activities, please check the school system which you feel excels in the purposes of education:

	Public Schools	Catholic Schools
Practical Courses (shops, home economics vocational courses, etc.)	100%	
Science and Math	95%	5%
Physical Culture (including corrective)	100%	
Athletics and Recreation	100%	
Public Speaking and Community Relations	100%	
Preparation for Public Life	100%	
Freedom of Thought and Evaluation	100%	
Objective Testing and Vocational Guidance	100%	
Objective and Unbiased Administration	100%	

3. Among students of Latin-American background are language difficulties more pronounced among

> Public school graduates   7%
> Catholic parochial graduates   93%

4. On entering public high school or college, how do children from Catholic parochial schools compare with those of public schools in subjects learned largely by rote (spelling, penmanship, arithmetic, reading, etc.)?

> Equal 50% Better 30% Worse 20%

5. In subjects requiring initiative in thought (social studies, composition, etc.)?

> Equal 27% Better 0 Worse 73%

6. Are your problems of moral (i.e., sexual) offenses greater among graduates of

> Public schools   9%
> Catholic parochial schools 91%

7. Are your problems of offenses regarding personal and property rights (i.e., assault and theft) greater among graduates of
> Public schools 20%
> Catholic parochial schools 80%

8. Do most Catholic children prefer their own parochial schools to the public schools?

> Yes 23%   No 77%

a. If the answer is "yes," to what do you attribute their decision?

Own wishes 0 Parental wishes 20% Church pressure 80%

9. Considering all the aspects of a well rounded education for success and good citizenship, is it your observation that young people are better prepared in

Catholic parochial schools 0   Public schools 100%

Some observations accompanying the answers also seem significant. From the Department of Education of the University of Minnesota: "My own experience with college students leads me to believe that generally the product of the public school is superior in terms of preparation than his peer in the parochial school."

A former professor of the School of Journalism of Northwestern University, Lawrence Martin, wrote, "I think that on the whole they (Catholic school graduates) were less well prepared for college than public school students. . . . My impression is also that students in our university coming for post-graduate work from Catholic colleges were inferior. This certainly applies to nuns studying in the summer school. . . . Out of five cases of plagiarism of themes that came my way, four of them were by Catholic students. In a school of journalism, we naturally regarded this offense as serious."

From the assistant director of admissions at a New England University: "I distinctly recall the director saying often that the university had found that the best students at parochial schools could not do work that those in the lower half of a class from most public high schools could do easily. . . . When I taught at the U. of —— I often discovered that the most poorly prepared students in my classes were from parochial schools."

A college professor in Missouri wrote: "Public school graduates excel generally (as they continue through high school); Catholic school children are inferior (in subjects requiring initiative in thought); parochial school pupils excel in habitual reactions such as the multiplication table, also in writing, a pure habit. But they are inferior in thought questions, including thought questions on *when* to multiply or *whether* to multiply or divide."

A high school principal bases his answers "on over thirty-four years of teaching and trying to guide public school pupils in elementary and secondary schools of Missouri, Colorado and Arizona. . . . They always answer 'yes, sir,' and 'no, sir' but otherwise they are, as a rule, not prepared in the subject matter as well as public school pupils. . . . Public school pupils, by all means, seem better prepared to pursue high school courses."

A retired Phoenix elementary school principal stated: "My experience was with the children from five to fifteen years. Many transfers were made from the parochial schools to the public schools during my work in Phoenix. In this time I found that practically all of them were one-half to a year behind the public school children. . . . I taught in New Jersey before coming to Arizona. At the school, other teachers and I were of the opinion that the graduates of a parochial school were inferior in preparation and we didn't like to get them in our school."

From an official of one of the West Coast's largest school systems. "We observe some frustrations in Catholic students. Lack social adjustment. Lack broadness of experience and viewpoint. Sometimes better prepared in concentrated area but not well adjusted persons . . .

about seventy-eight percent are Catholic in our problem children."

From a teacher in a very large California system: "Students from Catholic parochial schools *do not* have as good habits, morals, etc."

Also from California:

"As a high school teacher, I have reason to believe Catholic high schools expel their incorrigibles, who then attend public high schools and become discipline cases. . . .

"Where I taught, in a poor district, parochial school children during the depression could not pay the parochial tuition and came en masse to public school. The comparison favored the public schools."

"I taught for a time in the California State reform school. By far the larger part were Catholic."

Catholic students "are no better scholastically. Some, at first, are like 'scared rabbits' but soon develop into discipline problems. They do not come to me ahead in their work . . . I have received some children from such schools who are very good citizens, but never any to *my knowledge* who were ahead in their work."

"When I had Mexican children, children from parochial schools were generally at least a semester behind. Many of them proved to be discipline problems. Their religious training seemed to be apart from their daily living. . . . Many of the children from Catholic parochial schools have been such discipline problems that they are no longer wanted and so are forced to attend the public schools."

Etc., etc., etc.

These scattered evaluations are endorsed by Paul E. Flicker ("How Good are Our Schools") in the November,

1954, issue of the Bulletin of the National Association of Secondary School Principals (Vol. 38, No. 205, pp. 3-5). "When the facts are known, the public school graduates excel the private school graduates academically in their college performance."

He showed that, in 1954, in Harvard, Yale and Colgate Universities, even though only about half of the student bodies were from public schools, fully three-fourths of the students elected to the national honorary scholastic society, Phi Beta Kappa, were graduates of public schools. "In nine of the thirteen subject achievement and aptitude tests, students in the public schools excelled those from independent schools. . . . The above facts are given to show that in the aggregate where both public and private school graduates attend the same colleges, the academic honors, as shown to Phi Beta Kappa, go in greater numbers to public school graduates."

CHAPTER TEN

Recruitment of Shock Troop Teachers

The Catholic parochial school system could not exist without a steady supply of teaching priests and especially of teaching nuns. They are the self-immolating victims who literally sacrifice their lives in an attempt to draw all children who come to them to the Catholic Church. They are, to the greatest degree, responsible for the loyalty of that minority who do remain true and especially those who become the active "shock troopers."

It is important to know how the Church recruits the raw material of this vast teaching army and how it trains them, especially how narrowly it trains them.

I have already told that I was enticed to the seminary in Santa Barbara by the descriptions of swimming in the ocean and picnics and hikes to the mountains, accompanied by a very vague notion that I could help save souls. I was, of course, loyal to the Catholic Church. I could conceive of no other.

It took the passing of the years to weld the steel bands of obedience and fear.

The teaching priests and nuns of America are in reality a "captive army." Technically a Catholic boy or girl "freely" thrills to the ideals of the Order and the Church. After years of preparation, he "voluntarily" pronounces the vows of poverty, chastity and obedience which bind him forever to the service of the hierarchy. He may be legally free to the moment he takes his vows; but, in my experience, his mental freedom had been destroyed years before.

Those who boast so strongly of this "freedom" of priests and nuns and who condemn so ruthlessly a priest who leaves because he feels he was seduced in his "infancy" are the first to condemn the oriental custom of child marriages or parental arrangements of marriages.

Not a state in the union will permit youngsters to marry at the age they are encouraged to enter seminaries and convents. And the curtain descends on their minds the moment they enter—not when they take their final vows. That ceremony is an anti-climax.

The hierarchy concentrates on convincing youngsters before adolescence and the years of puberty awaken them to the realization that not only the future life offers promise of happiness. The lead article of the 1955 "Vocation" issue of the Arizona REGISTER (March 11, 1955) states: "The fifth, sixth, seventh and eighth grades appear to be the time when God makes known to children a vocation to serve Him as a priest, a brother or a sister. . . . According to the Very Rev. John Martin, M.M., answers to questionnaires showed that more than fifty per cent of those who enter Maryknoll seminaries made up their minds in the fifth grade to be priests. . . . Father Martin points out that the policy of starting the training of boys for the priesthood in prep seminaries at an early age is not something new. The Holy See has advocated it for centuries."

The parochial school system has expanded so rapidly that there is a disturbing shortage in the "vocations," particularly in the teaching Orders, of both men and women.

To increase the number of children giving their lives to "God," the hierarchy has set up a recruitment program similar to that of the Army, Navy, Marines and Air Force.

Bishops establish Vocation Councils composed of priests and nuns, who conjure up the most effective ways of attracting parochial school pupils. Some religious orders have vocation experts who tour their schools, appealing to the teenagers with revival-type emotional appeals; and, if distances are not too great, inviting all interested youngsters to a personal tour of the seminary or "mother house."

Most ecclesiastical training centers are in dream settings in the mountains, on lake shores, or on the ocean. Many of them are remodeled pretentious estates of the distressed rich. The opportunities for hiking, fishing, swimming and the pride and security of great properties and tremendous buildings have a powerful appeal for poor Catholic boys and girls (especially the children of immigrants) who live in "fringe" neighborhoods, who have to sell papers and mow lawns to help their families eat, and whose closest approach to an estate is the corner ball park.

Add to this the prodding of an ambitious mother (particularly, Irish) who sees in the priesthood or sisterhood a vicarious assumption into an aristocracy that enables her to look down on those who achieve recognition by money or mere worldly possessions.

Questionnaires are circulated among the immature youngsters, supposedly evaluating the response to various vocations. Those who indicate even a remote interest in the priesthood or sisterhood are concentrated upon with the personalized attention of the local priest or nun who is the "vocation director."

Once a year, along with Fire Prevention Week, National Hospital Week, National Home Week, the Roman Catholic observes National Vocation Week. Of all the thousands of occupations open to American youth, the only vocation concentrated on is the "religious" life.

Catholic papers (especially those in the REGISTER chain, with circulation in the millions) carry advertisements from Orders of priests, nuns and brothers outdoing each other in their appeals. The feature stories spotlight the various garbs of nuns, the happiness of self-sacrifice, the opportunity for service in school, hospital and foreign mission. Beautiful nuns vicariously satisfying their instincts by nursing little children are offset by pictures of handsome priests building new monasteries in the wilderness.

Through it all, of course, runs the theme that this call is from *Christ personally*. The impression is left that lack of response might involve a rejection of grace, or as we were told, the "pearl of great price." A generous acceptance will give happiness, security, service in Christ's army on earth—all this and heaven, too.

Even the Jesuits, who usually get their candidates from their own high schools, try to develop early vocations.

The following are letters to the editor of the magazine, *The Jesuit* (January, 1954).

From Pennsylvania:

Reverend and dear Father,
I am in the sixth grade and studying very hard so that I may come to India with you. I told my mother and she said it would be very nice if I could go. I have been praying for you very often. Please write soon.

> Your altar boy friend,
> William.

From New Jersey:

Dear Father,
Being interested in a religious vocation, I would like to have some information on the Jesuit Order. I am eleven years old and in Parochial School. I would also be interested in your magazine *The Jesuit*. Send it monthly to my home. Enclosed is one dollar donation so that I may be a member of the Jesuit Seminary Guild. Thank you and God bless you.

> George.

From Maryland:

Dear Father,
I am Ronald and would like to be a priest. I would like to receive your vocation notes and your magazine. I found out about you through Harry. With hopes of becoming good friends, I remain,

> Sincerely yours,
> Ronald.

Protestants have no conception of the powerful emotional response that the Roman Catholic doctrine of the

Eucharist or the Blessed Sacrament elicits in boys and girls when they have entered convents and seminaries.

They are taught that Jesus Christ is physically inside the tabernacle door on the center of the altar. The sacrament is not a symbol, or a reminder, but the actual living presence of the divine Christ and the very loving and lovable Jesus. The relationship developed is a very intimate, personal one; as though He were there for the one alone and all other seminarians did not exist. He does not leave when the Mass is finished. He remains night and day and seems particularly close when visited alone. He is ready to counsel, to strengthen, to love and particularly to be loved. There results a complete personalized sublimation of the budding urges of adolescence.

There is almost a puppy-love quality in some of the doggerel composed by young nuns:

> I chanced to pass an open door
> One day, and stopped to count my pearls;
> I spread my kerchief loosely on my head
> (As not to mess my curls) . . .
>
> Why should I, of all mankind,
> Be chosen as Your Bride?
> There are so many better far
> Than I, in this world so wide . . .
>
> I put away my dancing shoes
> I straighten out my curls
> I left my ballerina gown
> And a lovely string of pearls.
>
> I creep up close to a gold white rail
> On a marble tile-like floor,
> Where I know my Love is waiting
> Behind a little door.

I'm here, Beloved—here to stay;
I'll be quite homesick, too,
For I've never been away;
But I'll stay close to you.

A Sisters' house mother gives this advice:

"Religious life is a career. The Sisters are career girls of Our Lord. The future for them is a glorious eternity; and this career, my friend, is the real social security for heaven. So you see, the religious life is really *the career* of all careers. . . . Go to the tabernacle and seek the help of the One Whom you will serve as a Sister. He, Jesus, the son of God, will be your own Bridegroom, and it is He Who can whisper the answer to your question, 'Shall I be a Sister?' "

In religious orders for women, this personal emotional feeling for Christ is formalized in a wedding ceremony and many nuns wear wedding rings.

"What Must I Do?" by Sister Mary Paul Reilly, O. S. B. (Order of St. Benedict) is a presentation of the nun's life for girls interested in joining the convent. The chapter on admission to the congregation is entitled the "Bride of Christ."

When you do rise at seven-thirty, the sun is streaming into the dormitory and the birds are hurrying you along by the urgency of their chirping. You are reminded of your First Communion morning, and you surrender again to the same wonderment that possessed you then. The impression is strengthened by the atmosphere in the sewing room where your bridal gowns are waiting. The older Sisters pat and pin and inquire about results in subdued whispers. You are the center of everyone's pleased and proud attention. You remember Mother on that day so long ago as she warned teasing

Bob, "Let your sister alone now, she's supposed to be thinking about Jesus." As if anyone could distract you from Him today! You look around at your companions and know that they feel just as you do. A surge of love for them all wells up in you, and you know that it is fully returned . . .

You move up the aisle slowly and kneel before him in the monastery. There is a dialogue in which you express publicly your desire to receive the habit. Then the acolyte brings a little basket and a pair of golden scissors. You mount the altar steps and some of your hair is clipped off. Mother Church, you reflect, is woman enough to know what that will cost, even though the last of your permanent did unfurl three months ago. You take a long last look at Enid's lustrous natural waves. Soon they will be hidden forever. The little basket is quite full when the Bishop finishes. Those shorn little locks Sister Sacristan said would be given to your mothers, who will probably treasure them for posterity.[1]

"Of course," you tell yourself meditatively, "the religious life is really a love affair. Our Lord proposes to us in calling us to the convent. In accepting we give up all material things so we can be wholly dependent on Him; we give up the joys of human love and family life so we can belong to Him alone."[2]

And on the day of the profession of vows, Sister Paul describes the emotional climax: "The drama of the Mass unfolds until at last our Lord comes to you flooding your soul with joy and peace. There are no words to express your love, so you rest in Him, confident that he will understand."[3]

But not all American Catholic parents succumb to the blandishments of the priests and nuns. Many resist bitterly the efforts to seduce their youngsters at such an early age from their homes into the monasteries, seminaries and convents. Many a Catholic father wants his son to take on the store, factory or law office that he has labored to build. Many a Catholic mother wants her daughter to experience the attentions, diversions and spontaneous joys that she herself enjoyed as a young woman.

Many Catholics want their children brought up as strict, devoted Catholics; but believe that God gave man life, sex and material things to be legitimately used, enhanced and enjoyed. They cannot picture such enjoyment if their sons and daughters are weighted down by the vows of poverty, chastity and obedience.

The recent smoldering rebellion of American Catholic parents *threatens* to dry up the siphoning of Catholic youngsters to man the ever forced expansion of Catholic Church plants, schools and hospitals of America.

The hierarchy recognizes this danger. It warns little school children of the expected opposition of their parents, coaches them on how to answer parental objections and, if necessary, to defy them, because "obedience is due first to God, then to parents."

The booklet *Many are Called,* by Rev. Godfrey Poage, C. P. (Paulist) with an imprimatur by Cardinal Stritch of Chicago, and published in 1955 by the Catechetical Guild Educational Society of St. Paul, Minnesota, is an interesting example of one method of alleviating the shortage of vocations.

The author quotes a survey conducted by the Jesuit, Thomas S. Bowdern, among four thousand and fourteen young priests and nuns. Fifty-nine per cent of the men and seventy-two per cent of the nuns admitted parental pressure or opposition to their embracing the "religious" life. The opposition "ranged all the way from simple ridicule to downright physical violence." (My own experience was similar in dealing with families whose children wanted to enter religious life.)

"Only about a third of all the prospects I have interviewed during vocational campaigns, school programs and retreats have acknowledged any help or encouragement from their parents. Fully two-thirds of all the young men and women have admitted a measure of opposition from parents and relatives the moment they spoke about going to a seminary or convent." [4]

Personally I believe that active encouragement and pressure from parents upon their children to enter seminaries and convents is strongest among the Irish-Americans. The tradition has been obvious in Ireland and carries over to this country.

Fr. Poage lists and "refutes" forty-two objections that Catholic parents can and do have against giving their children to the Church. He admits that this is "far from being a comprehensive listing of the arguments."

The most important Catholic objections and the way Catholic parochial school children are taught to answer them should interest American Protestants and also Catholics who may have yet to face this crisis.

The admitted first and most frequent Catholic parental objection is that parochial school children in the eighth grade or early high school are "too young and immature to make the decisions involved in foreswearing normal life, particularly marriage, and the freedom to earn one's living in a competitive world."

The "vocational" directors insist that about fourteen is the ideal age for a boy or girl to make the decision. Fr. Poage quotes Fr. Francis Xavier Maynard, O. F. M., director of the Seraphic Society for Vocations, as saying that psychology indicates that the child should plan his vocation during *"the time between the ending of puberty and the beginning of adolescence."* (Italics ours) Here a child is best able to decide what he or she wants to be and do. Later on there is no such time of calm decision, for other forces come to bear upon the child and he or she begins to vacillate." [5]

An endorsement of this age for entering a seminary was given by Fr. Herman Doerr, O. F. M., the Vocational Director of the Franciscan Fathers' Sacred Heart Province. He is quoted by the Arizona (Catholic) REGISTER, July 29, 1955, as telling the American Franciscan Society for Vocations that it is better for a boy of fourteen to enter a seminary than to wait until he is eighteen and has completed high school.

In answering the parental objection to taking the child away from home while so young, Fr. Poage says, "The first part of this argument is quite hard to refute, since it is a half truth. Certainly boys and girls at fourteen or fifteen years of age do not realize what the priesthood, brotherhood or sisterhood really entails. (I was fifteen and the oldest of a class of more than thirty. Author's note.) But they can know at that age whether or not they want to find out about such a life for God." [6] He continues that even at "eighteen or nineteen the young man or woman knows little about the nature of the religious life." This is a fact that every ex-priest or ex-nun would readily confirm. But he justifies their ignorance by saying that such teenagers know just as little of marriage and still get married.

If the fourteen-year-old ("between puberty and ado-

lescence") doubts whether he should choose the priesthood or marriage, he should try the priesthood first.
"When a youth is in doubt as to whether God calls to
marriage or the religious state, it is never prudent to
choose marriage first . . . with the intention of attempting
the religious state if one does not find happiness in marriage. Rather one should investigate the religious life,
and if one finds happiness there, then one has found the
proper state. If one does not find happiness in a seminary
or convent, then marriage must be the vocation." [7]

There are two subtle fallacies in Fr. Poages' reasoning.
He forgets that the seminary is not merely a *trial* of an
acquaintanceship with the priesthood as far as the fourteen-year-old Catholic boy is concerned. It is not an
investigation on his part as to the desirability of spend-
ing all his life in theology, celibacy and ritual even when
admittedly young ("between puberty and adolescence").
He is too young to evaluate the priesthood. The seminary
also gives an opportunity to the hierarchy for an intense
indoctrination of the pliable youngsters' mind while in
physical seclusion. They are constantly taught the sanctity and desirability of the priestly life and the worldli-
ness of marriage, with its consequent pitfalls to salvation.

Fr. Poage also overlooks, in his statement that youngsters of eighteen know as little of marriage as they do
of the priesthood, that even eighteen-year-olds, much less
fourteen-year-olds, are neither solicited nor encouraged
to marry. However, if they do, they are still following
the normal course of nature and the traditional pattern
of all of their forbears.

Another Catholic parental objection to their children
stepping from grammar school into a monastery is that

they should "see the world first." By this, well-meaning parents feel that, before such an irrevocable decision, their children should travel a trifle, associate with adolescent boys and girls, get a job, and, in general, experience the aspects of life that they will forego in the convent or monastery.

Fr. Poage consoles Catholic parents: "When it is a case of parents who are afraid that their children will not know the facts of life before they take the vow of chastity, it is a much simpler situation. All that is needed is an explanation of how in the seminary or convent their youngsters will get the whole truth about human love and sex—but from God's viewpoint. The only thing they don't get is a sordid or prejudiced approach. All seminarians or novices are better informed before their vows than most couples on the verge of matrimony." [8]

It should be quite unnecessary to state that no ex-priest or ex-nun would agree with the above statements.

Other parental objections considered and "answered" are: "Too much pressure is exerted on parochial school children by priests and nuns"; "My child won't be happy in a convent or a monastery"; "The life of a priest or nun is so hard"; "My child's talents would be wasted in the priesthood"; "My boy is not good enough for the priesthood"; "My child's personality will be stifled"; "Children have obligations towards their parents," etc.

When Catholic parents will not accept the answers to these and other objections, Catholic children and parents are taught that the Roman Catholic Church represents God and that, as such, loyalty to the Church comes before loyalty to parents.

"When parents rashly contradict the divine invitation

and refuse permission for their children to enter the service of God, the *children can go without parental approval.* There is no question of disobedience, for when parents go against the superior will of God they cannot demand submission from their children.

"When dealing with these parents, I try to point out to them that they are on very shaky ground when they start talking about 'obligation' and hinting that their children are 'sinning against obedience.' If there is any sin, it is on the part of the parents!

"Obedience is due first to God, then to parents. Accordingly, when there is a conflict, children must first follow the divine will.

"St. Alphonsus Luquori, in his *Homo Apostolicus,* says: 'Parents, who without a just and certain cause prevent their children from entering the religious state, cannot be excused from *mortal* sin; and not only parents, but anyone who prevents another from following a religious vocation sins mortally.

"This is a very hard doctrine but one that should certainly be emphasized with many of our modern parents. They should certainly be reminded also of what the Fathers of the Council of Trent decreed in their 25th session: 'Let anyone who, without just cause, prevents another from embracing the religious state be anathema!' " [9]

I have had many letters from frantic parents, Catholic and Protestant, whose children have been literally seduced into convents and seminaries, asking me for help. There is none. The child must see for himself.

After the curtain that descends has cut off contact with the modern world, very little light can seep through.

Even before I left the priesthood, during the period of my growing disillusionment, whenever I heard or read of a boy or girl taking vows, I could think of nothing but the ancient god Moloch into whose yawning, fire-belching maw, virgins were periodically hurled to satisfy the god or the high priests. In the end result, what's the difference between the horrible death and the frustrating lingering entombment in a monastery or convent?

As important as the Church's method of seducing its teaching force is the system of training them to teach future Catholics and, particularly, the hard core of its "shock troopers."

The boys and girls who enter seminaries and convents come to their teachers in a sense "predigested."

Practically all have been through Catholic grammar schools. They have had the usual curriculum, colored with the usual Catholic infiltration. They have been subjected to the same intense, rigid, if confusing, moral code and have lived up to it; or they wouldn't be this far. Their very presence proves that the emotional panoply of medals, statues, rituals and devotions, particularly to Mary, have been very successful.

They are the embryonic elite of the "shock troops" of the Church militant.

What is needed now is time—time to indoctrinate them with the lore of higher Catholicism, with the semblance, at least, of a college education, with Catholic history (as the Church sees it and wants it taught), with the working tools of their profession, Catholic scripture, Catholic philosophy, Catholic moral theology and Catholic dogmatic theology, and time to drill young Americans in loyalty and obedience.

The usual seminary course for priests throughout the world lasts twelve or thirteen years.

The first four or five years resemble a liberal arts course, with the greatest emphasis on Latin. We studied also Greek, Spanish, German, Hebrew and, of course, English. In my day, the scientific subjects were only schematically touched upon. Religious subjects were not too strongly stressed in the classroom; but we lived in such an old world monastic atmosphere that this was not necessary.

The novitiate year (period of trial) follows. Here the young aspirant lives monasticism at its strictest—that the clerical superiors may see if he can take it. Mass, meditation, spiritual reading, classes on the history of the Order, recitation of the Divine Office and strict seclusion occupy the entire year before he takes his simple vows.

The next section of our training was the field of philosophy. In our case, it lasted two years and covered all the branches of scholastic philosophy and an alleged history of philosophy. These "history" books were, of course, written by Catholic authors; and we were not encouraged, in fact, were not permitted—to read the works of any non-Catholic philosophers. We were told that they were too "materialistic" and dangerous.

The main subjects in our final four years of indoctrination were dogmatic and moral theology. Our textbooks compressed into a few volumes the accumulated and passed-on beliefs concerning doctrine and behavior from the earlier teachers of the Church, plus the opinions of later theological authorities. Wherever possible, an attempt was made to bolster these beliefs with a Scripture argument. But this was not necessary. The doctors could always fall back on "tradition," which equaled the Bible as a source of revelation.

Canon Law was also considered an extremely important course in these years. It is the codified law of the Church of over two thousand laws, which bind clergy and laymen alike. One argument against devout Catholics being elected to an executive, judicial or law enforcement office in the United States, is Canon No. 120, which forbids Catholics around the world from hailing a priest before a court without the prior permission of his bishop.

We studied the Bible during those four years. The subject was called "exegesis." We tried to memorize the Catholic interpretation of controversial passages of the Scriptures, but were not permitted to read any Protestant Biblical studies.

It was taken for granted that all Catholic interpretations were true; because God preserves the one true Church from error. Any Protestant interpretation, such as thinking the "rock" might not mean St. Peter, must be certainly false.

The studies I pursued are substantially the same in all seminaries in the country. The nuns are prepared for their teaching work according to the pattern of their various organizations.

Throughout the formative years of the priesthood or sisterhood, a jealous mother watches every mental step. Every textbook is written by a Catholic. All knowledge of Protestant and other world religions comes to him predigested by a Catholic author. The great doors of the *Index of Forbidden Books* bar his way to the libraries of the world's thinkers. He is taught to accept and not to think.

The ex-Paulist priest, Rev. William Sullivan, incomparably expresses this thought:

". . . The Church is jealous of inner light and private leading. She must choose the road and count the steps. On her arm the seeker must forever lean; only with her must he converse by the way; and at her command he must reject ideas of the mind and attractions of the moral sense, if she disapproves them. She keeps vigilance over his reading, keeps guard over the door of his studies, and stands with a warning look beside him as he forms his judgments of history, of sacred texts, of philosophy, and even of devotional theory and practice.

". . . But let him be irked by her perpetual tutelage and fretted by her unrelaxing hold upon him, and he soon will know how harsh and swift her stroke can be, and how well practiced in smiting, as in blessing, is her dread right hand."[10]

Philip Wylie points out in the intellectual cud chewing of William Percival Gamit in *Night Unto Night*, that the Roman Church is the conscience of all its students. It controls their thoughts and visits excommunications on those who presume to *think* (*quicumique censuerit*) at variance with it. The oratorical debates that take place among seminarians and in convents are merely mental gymnastics. The students dare not deviate from the "party line" of Rome.

The hard core of the young priest's or nun's mind lies cast in the mould. Only the fringe area could flirt with modern science, economics, commerce or philosophy, and that only so long as its gambolings do not conflict with it.

Every teaching priest in America takes the following solemn oath: "I firmly embrace and receive each and every teaching, defined, asserted and declared by the unerring magisterium of the Catholic Church, especially those doctrines directed against the errors of our times . . . I condemn the error of those who hold that it is even possible for Catholic teachings to be unhistorical . . . I damn and reject the opinion that a learned Catholic has a dual personality—one that of a believer, the other that of a historian . . . I promise to reject in its entirety that error through which modernists contend that 'tradition' is not divine, or, which is far worse, interpret it in a pantheistic sense so that we have only bald and simple fact, conforming to the common facts of history; and that the school founded by Christ and his apostles has endured through subsequent ages by the industry, solicitude and genius of man. Furthermore I most firmly hold fast to the faith of the Fathers and I shall hold fast to the last breath of my life . . . All of this I swear that I shall preserve faithfully, wholly and sincerely and shall guard it inviolate and never in teaching, in preaching, in speaking or in writing shall I in any detail deviate from it. So I promise, so I swear, so help me God and these the holy Gospels of God."[11]

This "Oath Against Modernism," by decree of the Holy Office (March 22, 1918), is still binding and must accompany the Profession of Faith enjoined by Canon Law No. 1406 on all priests, especially teachers, preachers and confessors.

The illusion of intellectual and educational freedom is created by permitting some priests and nuns to do postgraduate work in state universities. But they are merely innocent colts frisking in the corral, while the seasoned ecclesiastical cowhands sit in their clerical levis on the fence rails and plan the most effective way of breaking them to years under the saddle. While studying in state universities, they live in convents and monasteries. They attend meditation and Mass before entering the classroom and return to monastic prayer, the "Divine Office" and the cloistered atmosphere, when the lectures are over.

The liberalism of a state university rarely penetrates. If it does, the treatment is quick and drastic. An example is that of the "worker priests" of France. These self-sacrificing, idealistic men went into the slums and factories to live poverty with the poor and not merely preach the virtues of the vow of poverty in the comparative luxury of the monastery.

They saw so much of the festering filth of society's back alleys that they began to understand the lure of Communism to those who had nothing to lose. They wrote and spoke what they saw. The Vatican ordered them back into their monasteries, exiled their leaders and threatened the recalcitrants with excommunication. In 1957, years after the ultimatum of the Vatican, several of those priests had still refused obeisance.

Not only the priests who occupy the podium in a high school or college classroom are considered teachers in the Catholic educational system. For in that system, as we have shown, the classroom is only the formal aspect of teaching. In the grammar school system, the burden of that task falls on the nuns.

The priest educator functions just as vitally in the Sunday pulpit, in the confessional, in personal counselling and in instructing converts.

As a young priest, I taught catechism classes in the early grades of St. Mary's Grammar School in Phoenix. The nuns trained the children to chant by rote, exactly as I had been trained, the simple assumed "truths" of the catechism; e.g., "Has Christ established more than one church? Christ has established but one church as He has taught but one Faith . . . the Roman Catholic Church alone is the Church established by Christ, and hence all are bound to be members of that Church." My function was to examine the youngsters on certain days of the week to make sure that the nuns were drilling them properly.

I was promoted to the status of religion instructor in the girls' high school. It was presumed that the nuns were not as well trained in Catholicism and theology as were the priests. High school students might ask questions beyond the ability of the nuns to answer. It was my duty to take the questions of the advanced catechism and to elaborate on them up to the point of the girls' interest and capacity to understand.

The height of my personal teaching career was as a faculty member of the staff of St. Joseph's Hospital School of Nursing in Phoenix. This continued for some years. I was the "professor" of religion, of ethics, and of psychology.

Only the Roman Catholic girls were forced to attend the religion class. It was similar to that at the girls' high school, but a bit more advanced. The girls were older. Their moral problems and questions had also advanced. They were torn between the eruption of their own physical desires and the attempts of the nuns to make them live a semi-cloistered life. While on nursing duty in the hospital, they were in constant contact with men, many of them gentlemen, but just as many who exhibited unres-

trained lecherous desires at the sight of these neatly uni-
formed, healthy, exuberant, friendly girls. One of the great
problems in nursing schools concerns the number of student nurses who fall in love with patients and never finish
their training. Being the chaplain of the student nurses
as well as their religion instructor, I had the opportunity
to advise many of them. My counsel was to postpone their
marriages till graduation or, if they had already secretly
married, to keep it secret from the officials of the nursing
school. Later, when I was the head of a hospital operating
its own nursing school, I gave our girls the same advice.
I have never been able to understand why students should
live as celibate nuns merely because they are studying
nursing.

I taught "psychology for nurses." More than half of the
girls were non-Catholic. Yet the course I was instructed
to teach, and I did, was the Aristotelian Thomistic concept of psychology embodied in what is called scholastic
philosophy. It was traditional Roman Catholic psychology, as taught in all American Roman Catholic colleges
and universities. Fortunately, I do not believe the courses
left any lasting impressions on the student nurses.

The subject matter which did, in many cases, leave a
harmful impression on those girls was the course I taught
them in "medical ethics." Under that noble sounding title,
I drilled into those budding nurses (about half of them
Protestants) the Roman Catholic law as it pertained to
surgical procedures, when the life of a mother or her unborn child might hang in the balance. I taught to Catholic
and non-Catholic nurses alike, what I had been taught—
that no surgical procedure could legitimately be used that
might save the mother at the expense of the child. I

taught them that abortion under any and all circumstances, regardless of state laws, was murder. I taught them that sterilization of man or woman, regardless of health, finances, or mental instability or impending breakdown, could never be permitted. I taught them that giving birth control information, no matter how much it might seem necessary, was a mortal sin. I also emphasized the sinfulness of "cooperation" in sin. They, as nurses, in assisting in surgery at an abortion, or a sterilization or fitting a diaphragm were in just as much danger of hell as the doctor.

I taught these girls that, in case of the death of a pregnant woman, the baby or fetus, if possible, was to be baptized "in utero." I taught them that every dying baby, regardless of the religion of the parents, if unbaptized, was to be baptized into the Catholic Church. The assumption was, I profoundly told the girls, that if the parents had any sense, they would know that the Catholic Church is the true church and would want their babies baptized. This same line of logic was used in encouraging the nurses to call me or another priest to give the Catholic last rites to all patients brought in unconscious.

Since opening our hospital and especially since leaving the priesthood, I have attempted to atone for this arrogant presumptuousness. We permit abortions and sterilizations when done according to law. We do not tolerate any baptisms of babies unless the parents request it. And even if the unconscious emergency victim is O'Brien or Gonzales, no priest is permitted near the patient unless a relative requests it. We have also joined with the Planned Parenthood group and have a Birth Control Clinic in our hospital.

I was a teacher in the pulpit for fifteen years. In the early years I explained Catholic doctrines, as I was expected to do. I even occasionally painted the abysmal fiery tortures of purgatory and hell. I explained the Catechism, in accordance with the bishops' sermon schedule; even though it seemed a rather moronic thing to do while the children in the congregation were hearing this every day of the week and the adults had heard it ad nauseam. It was an easy thing for a priest to do, requiring no imagination or literary creative ability whatever.

As the years slipped by and doubts multiplied and I was free in my own little church to speak without restriction, I preached more and more of love of God rather than the fear of God and his thunderbolts. I preached simple little moral sermons. These poor Negro and Mexican people were burdened enough with racial discrimination and the depression not to have to hear more grief in church on Sundays.

I was also a teacher as a confessor. The mechanics of going to confession comprise a humble supplication on the part of the penitent (the one confessing); then the recitation of sins. The priest is then to probe deeper. He should find if the person has confessed all his serious (mortal) sins; if there are any mitigating or complicating circumstances (for example, sexual relations between an unmarried man and woman constitute fornication; if one is married, adultery; if one is a priest or nun, sacrilege). He is then supposed to give the penitent a moral lecture reprimanding him according to the severity of his sins and making him promise not to sin again. Then he gives absolution.

I dutifully observed this protocol when I was first ordained. Again, with the years, I gradually learned a few facts of life. When a human promises never to sin again he is a liar, so I quit asking people to make this promise.

The most commonly confessed sin by adults was birth control. I was hearing confessions on weekends through those years; and, during the week, I was developing venereal clinics and a maternity clinic. Many a woman we delivered had six, eight or ten children and could hardly feed any of them. What we needed was more birth control, not a condemnation of it. I adopted the policy of never reprimanding a person in the confessional for the practice of birth control. Word of my leniency spread and I became known as the "birth control priest."

I started my Phoenix ministry in 1934. Within a year, I was working in my spare time on the south side of the city. There I was up against the stark ugly reality of people living, or rather starving, in a jungle. Unpaved streets, no electricity, gas or running water in their hovels. There was no public health, no maternity care and no interest that these outcasts should have care. The sum total of their sanitary facilities was usually a hole in the ground.

It was difficult for me to concentrate on the abstractions of papal infallibility, the assumption of the Virgin Mary or the pronouncements of the Council of Trent when people were starving around me.

I no longer desired to excel as a teacher of the "shock troopers." I listlessly went through the motions in the classroom, in the pulpit, and in the confessional. In 1947 and 1948, this shifting of interest from the "spiritual to the material" (as the hierarchy said) became a very serious source of friction between myself and my ecclesiastical peers. By that time they did not consider me an asset to the Church Militant.

In reviewing these aspects of my career as a teacher, I can find little in which to take much pride. As far as contact with reality is concerned, I might just as well have been plucked out of the Middle Ages.

CHAPTER ELEVEN

Training of The Shock Troops

It is true that very many products of the Catholic school system leave the Church openly and definitely. Many others give up the practice of Catholicism, but nominally remain Catholics. Others, and a very large number they are, keep up the external formalities of their faith, but are certainly not subservient to their clergy.

There still remains that hard core of bishops, priests, nuns, and the laity whom we call the "shock troops" of the Church Militant.

They are the people who have remained impervious to the "snares of the evil one" and blindly accept everything their clergy tells them.

I have tried to explain the mental, moral and emotional indoctrination to which I was subjected both in the elementary schools and in the seminary. I have tried to show that this same pattern obtains in all Catholic schools.

The Church, however, is not content with the intense drilling of its school system. She has already lost too many on their way through. She uses every possible means to preserve the loyalty they feel. She must also continue the indoctrination; so that she may use them on one or more of the many fronts through which she is constantly striving to expand her power and her numbers in America.

One approach is the attempt to enroll devout Catholics in one or more of the host of Catholic societies in America. The hierarchy wants its people, insofar as it is possible in our pluralistic society, to associate with Catholics. This eliminates controversial religious arguments. It eliminates discussions of books that might be on the ecclesiastical black list. It also provides a sense of strength and solidarity by giving them the illusion of great numbers within the Church.

The variety of societies for lay people within the Church is almost limitless.

The best advertised is the Knights of Columbus. It numbers approximately a million members. To belong, a man must be not only a Catholic, but a practicing Catholic. He must confess and receive communion at least once a year. This Order was founded by a priest with a primary purpose of satisfying the lodge desires of those who were tempted to join the Masons. Its local lodges assume various Catholic projects. Nationally it spends a great deal of money in many magazines with catchy half-truth advertisements designed to enroll Protestants in correspondence convert courses. It claims that these are very successful.

The Catholic Daughters of America constitute the "Eastern Star" of Catholic womanhood.

The Holy Name Society is generally preferred by parish clergy over the K. C.; because each unit is tied to a parish, whereas the K.C. frequently covers a whole city. The priests can more easily use the parish group for their own purposes and can also control their officers and policies. The Holy Name Society is also more religious and holds processions (sometimes city-wide) and pageants to continue to instill all the faithful with the greatness and sanctity of the Church. Its members are usually very docile "shock troopers" and respond for the boycotting of a book store or a theatre that defies the hierarchy.

A sample of how they are drilled and prepared for such a mission is shown in the following proud account of the mobilization of Pittsburgh to carry out the completely un-American censorship of books because the Catholic hierarchy doesn't like them:

After five years of comparatively meager success in attempting to combat the overwhelming task of ridding the stores and newsstands of objectionable literature, the Holy Name Societies of the Pittsburgh Diocese have developed a new approach to the problem. . . .

Each parish Holy Name Society conducted a survey to determine the location of all stores and newsstands where literature is sold within the parish limits. . . . Committee members employed in the downtown business section surveyed that area during lunch hours and shopping trips.

The diocesan spiritual director and members of the diocesan committee spent many evenings phoning the men whose names were suggested. Each man was asked to respond to the urgent request of the Most Reverend Bishop for an effective approach to the problem of indecent literature.

The next step was to mail to the visitor a kit which contains the following:

1. A letter signed by the diocesan spiritual director thanking the visitor in the name of the Most Reverend Bishop for accepting the assignment and stressing the importance of the project.

2. A list of rules for conducting the visit. An important rule is that each visitor take a companion with him.

3. An official identification card.

4. Two copies of the printed list of objectionable publications.

5. Two report forms.

6. A specially prepared prayer card, approved by the Bishop; and a medal of St. Maria Goretti, patroness of purity.

7. A N.O.D.L. (National Organization for Decent Literature) Poster for the proprietor's window. This poster is awarded to those proprietors who show evidence of complete and continued cooperation.

When the quarterly reports are received at the Central Office, notations are made on the card records, indicating the date of the visit, whether the proprietor is cooperating or promises to cooperate, whether cooperating fully or partially, or refuses to cooperate. Duplicate copies of the reports are sent to the deanery chairmen, so that they may be informed of the progress of the campaign in their respective areas.

The number of stores handling literature in the diocese is estimated at 1,000. The surveys uncovered about 880 such stores, the majority of which are visited regularly. Reports received and tabulated to date show that about 70 per cent of the proprietors are cooperating, or promise to cooperate fully; about 15 per cent are cooperating partially; and about 15 per cent refused to cooperate.

The reports are reviewed by the diocesan committee. Suggestions and recommendations of the store visitors are considered and referred to the diocesan spiritual director for decision as to appropriate action.

Another society deserving of special mention is the Newman Club. It is a very successful organization whose principal purposes are to preserve the loyalty of devout students and to elicit the dedication of young "shock troopers" when they are emotionally most susceptible.

I pointed out earlier that one serious source of leakage was the attendance of Catholics at non-Catholic colleges and universities. The Newman Club was devised to combat this leakage. The clubs exist in public and private non-Catholic colleges and universities across the country. Many clubs have elaborate structures adjacent to the campuses containing a chapel, auditorium, kitchen, classrooms and counselling rooms. The students are urged to attend daily Mass and communion, and take an active part in club academic discussions designed to counteract anything "subversive" heard in the classrooms. Every club is, of course, administered by a priest. These chaplains are carefully chosen for their own loyalty and dedication as "shock troopers."

There are Catholic clubs to provide a church haven for the faithful in practically every trade or profession. A few are: Catholic Editors Association, Catholic Hospital Association, Catholic Teachers Association, Catholic Writers Guild, Catholic Actors Guild, Catholic War Veterans, Catholic Postal Employees, Eucharistic League, Guild of Catholic Lawyers, Catholic Trade Unionists Association and, in larger cities, Catholic firemen and policemen's associations.

A common characteristic of most of these is the "communion breakfast." In large cities, after the Mass the group marches publicly, as a show of strength, to a restaurant or hotel where after breakfast an inspiring speech is given by some prominent Catholic, frequently a lawyer, judge, or businessman. Their emotional batteries are recharged and they go forth rededicated.

The same reason exists for the conventions held by these societies. Mass, sermons, and inspirational talks are interwoven with scientific or trade discussions, again to impress the group with the Church's impregnability.

The most concentrated session of Catholic indoctrination for the real faithful and the "shock troopers" is the retreat. Priests and nuns must make a retreat each year. Canon Law, religious order regulation, and diocesan statutes all require it. Lay people are strongly urged to do so. The retreat for priests and nuns lasts from seven to ten and, in some Orders, up to thirty days. During this period, the retreatants are supposed to observe silence. They may not carry out any of their parochial, teaching, or nursing duties. Special religious services are held during the day. The retreat master, a priest, is the "captain of the ship" during these days. He preaches several sermons each day, usually with much emphasis on sin, purgatory and hell. In their spare time, the retreatants are to read only spiritual books and meditate intensely on their own weaknesses and sins. At the close of the retreat, every one is expected to make a soul-searching confession.

"Retreat houses" for lay people are being built across the country. The main differing characteristic of the lay retreats is that they have to be held on weekends to accommodate working people.

The supercolossal Hollywood-type spectacle of Catholicism is the national or international Eucharistic Congress. Preparations are made many months in advance. Cardinals, archbishops, and bishops are gathered from everywhere. All the splendor of ancient liturgical pageantry is utilized. The biggest stadium in the area or the country is obtained. Advance advertising goes on long before the event in the best tradition of a circus. And when it arrives, Catholics of all ranks gather by the thousands, usually at least a hundred thousand. Outdoor pontifical Masses are said, evening candlelight services are held. The people are told that one person with a candle is nothing, but one hundred thousand candles could yield a mighty light. Again the message is gotten over that the Church is the most powerful and unshakable force in the nation. The loyalty and devotion of the "storm troopers" have been renewed and intensified.

Of the more intellectual tools used to hold and further train the "storm troopers," probably the most successful is the Catholic press. This press boasts of weekly circulations in the many millions. *Our Sunday Visitor* is a raucous insulting weekly tabloid, sold in practically every church in the United States. It appeals to the faithful of limited intelligence. It undoubtedly keeps them in line and helps provide the manpower for boycotts and picket lines.

The diocesan weeklies hit a higher intellectual level. The most powerful is the REGISTER chain, published in Denver and adapted for very many dioceses. These are principally religious newspapers. But they carry many columns, usually written by priests, repeating and re-emphasizing the Church's most common moral and doctrinal teachings, with frequent attempts to explain away shady points in history.

The National Organization for Decent Literature attempts to control paperbacks. The *Index* and the warning of priests keep subversive (i.e., critical) books out of devout Catholic hands.

The censorship which the hierarchy attempts to exercise over movies, radio and television has the same purpose.

The positive training sessions for the various fields of the Church's community efforts are called "Catholic Action." This has been defined as the "cooperation of the laity in the work of the hierarchy."

Some are taught in the social service courses of Catholic universities, others in the action classes in Newman Clubs and others in groups organized in many parishes. They are the lay leaders that the clergy can always tap.

Another method is for the pastor to call up one or more of his existing societies when a local crisis arises, such as the impending acceptance by the United Fund of a Planned Parenthood Group. The technique is to use the illusion of numerical strength.

The unquestioned leader of all Catholic social and political activities is the bishop. Some priests will assist him; and some are not interested but will go through the motions of cooperation to save their ecclesiastical hides.

Insofar as I know, the closest approach to formal political indoctrination in a Catholic institution is the "School of Foreign Service" in Georgetown University in Washington, D. C. Otherwise I believe the political pressure is exercised by bishops and priests as the occasion arises. I don't believe Catholic congressmen are aware of their role as "storm troopers" before they are elected. It is done afterwards.

The same holds true in State legislatures, county and city governments and the politics of school districts. The bishops have their nucleus of trained devotees, usually a few lawyers, doctors and well known business men who can privately put on the pressure, at least enough to scare most legislators or city councilmen. They can then call in the hoi polloi of the shock troopers to jam the galleries or the council chambers and convince the poor officials that the Church really controls the area. It is all usually a lie, of course.

CHAPTER TWELVE

Shock Troops in Action

There is obviously no possible way of knowing how many sincere, devoted, unselfish, dedicated Catholics there are in the United States. On the basis of my personal experience as a priest and as an observer of this situation for the past eleven years, I do not think that more than one-fourth of the Catholics of America would bestir themselves mentally, physically, or especially financially for the Holy Mother Church in case of any serious crisis.

A close friend, an ex-Catholic, who has been a student of the Roman Catholic picture in America for many years, feels that the hierarchy retains its hold on about half of the people who are exposed to the parochial school system through the university level. She agrees, of course, that the Church's claim to forty million members in the United States is as fictitious as the story of the Wizard of Oz.

Whatever the figure or whatever the percentage, the array of "shock troops," or, as the Church prefers to call

231

them, the "Church Militant," is impressive in numbers and in power in the United States. If there were a fraction as many Communists in the country, the nation would be shaken with fear for its security.

The startling but unrealized fact is that our nation's principles, traditions, and free institutions are just as much in danger as if these dedicated Catholics were Communists. The opposition to freedom of thought, freedom to read, freedom of speech is identical whether it comes from the Kremlin or the Vatican.

It is not only astounding but frightening to realize the growing controls with which these Catholic "shock troopers" have gradually and quietly been hamstringing this nation, suppressing its traditions and freedoms and paving the way for its goal to "make America Catholic."

The growing Roman Catholic control of America is such an insidious thing that most lay Catholics and even the bulk of the clergy are unaware of it. The bishops, the national Catholic Welfare Conference in Washington, and the Jesuits are certainly master-minding it.

The Roman Catholic Church tries to function as a super government in the United States, as it actually does in the countries it completely controls. Examples are Spain, Portugal, Italy and most Latin-American nations. It feels that its doctrine, its concept of history, its code of morals and system of ethics are above the laws of this land. Its leaders, the cardinals and bishops, are conspicuously silent in the face of the Roman Catholic Sicilian Mafia's complete defiance of decency and morals in the promotion of prostitution, narcotics, gambling, and labor racketeering in America. The same bishops and archbishops who vociferously condemn a young Catholic girl for entering a beauty contest say nothing about the traffic in narcotics and whoredom so long as good Catholics run the business.

Attention is now being focussed in the press and other forms of public information about the possibility of a Roman Catholic President. But little attention has been drawn to the "shock troopers'" established inroads into Congress, government agencies, state, county and municipal governments.

The average Catholic knows practically nothing of his Church's laws as embodied in the 2414 statutes of the *Codex Juris Canonici* (the Code of Canon Law). The average Protestant knows less. The average Protestant cares less.

But he might care, in the face of a possible Roman Catholic President of the United States, if he realized that the Roman Catholic Canon Law sets itself above all laws of all nations and enforces upon all Roman Catholic officials of all nations the obligation of preserving the laws of Rome above the laws and constitutions that they are sworn to protect and observe.

Among many citable canons are #120 and #121 elevating the clergy above civil laws and declaring them immune to all nations' laws of military service.

Incidents occur around the world of Catholic officials being threatened with ex-communication if they dare arrest an ecclesiastic, such as happened in Haiti in mid-1959.

Stories occasionally break into print of priests defying state laws and declaring themselves subject only to their bishops, even in violation of civil statutes. This happened in Tucson, Arizona, in 1958, in a dispute between a priest and the Arizona Highway Commission. It happened in Virginia City, Nevada, in July, 1959, over an assault and battery charge.

Policemen and retired policemen can relate instances, ad nauseam, of priests in cities across the country violating the laws and either being protected by Catholic policemen, county attorneys, and judges, or defying these officers and getting away with it.

For the first time in American history, Roman Catholics now constitute the largest religious bloc in the Congress of the United States. The effect of this power is obvious in the actions of the Congress and the prejudicial religious favoritism of federal agencies.

Representative McCormack of Massachusetts has done yeoman service for the hierarchy. It has resulted in his receiving high honors from the Vatican. He is the one who engineered the bills through Congress, with all the Masonic congressmen strongly concurring, that gave over nine hundred thousand dollars to the Pope to repair the damage an American bomb accidentally did to the Vatican summer palace. The Lutherans lost out completely in not pressing for American funds to rebuild the churches destroyed by Americans in Germany.

Something over twenty million dollars was voted to rebuild Catholic institutions in the Philippines—again with McCormack handling the strategy so well that the Protestants concurred.

The abject subservience of American federal agencies to Roman Catholic control is unbelievable in a country that is supposed to be a democracy.

The Hill-Burton program of federal aid to hospitals is

one case in point. In their wildest untruthful exaggerated claims, Catholics do not constitute twenty-five per cent of the population. Ten per cent would be closer to the truth. Yet almost eighty per cent of all federal funds being given to non-profit church hospitals in America is being given to Catholic sisters' hospitals. And they are being operated according to the code of ethics of the Roman Catholic Church—not the laws of the United States of America, the various states or the code of the American Medical Association. A letter to one's congressman asking about the donation of the Hill-Burton millions will verify my statements.

For several years, our hospital has given the fullest possible cooperation to the Planned Parenthood Program of Phoenix. We furnish clinic space free of charge. We supply nurses, linens, telephone service, and everything else we can. Birth control is very important in our end of town, especially among the poor Catholics. Furthermore, my promotion of a birth control clinic as an ex-priest irritates the hierarchy—and this gives me much satisfaction.

In the expansion program of our outpatient area, we wanted to provide a new office for the executive secretary of the Planned Parenthood Foundation. I was tipped to describe it on the plans as "Office of Social Service Secretary" or "Mothers' Conference Room," if I expected to get the plans approved and federal Hill-Burton participation. I was told that there are enough Catholics in the U.S. Public Health Service (the agency administering the Hill-Burton funds) to stop construction of anything the Catholic hierarchy objects to—in the United States of America.

The U.S. Civil Service Commission is supposed to be in existence to guarantee the stability of employment of worthy civil servants. This is not always true—especially when the long arm of the Catholic hierarchy reaches in to destroy one of its recalcitrant priests who prefers the freedom of America to the blessings of the "one, true faith."

These following facts can be verified by a prominent firm of attorneys in Phoenix, as well as by many Masons, the Masonic Grand Lodge of Arizona, and the El Zaribah Shrine of Arizona.

Father M., one of my schoolmates in St. Anthony's Seminary of Santa Barbara, chose to quit the priesthood. He needed a job. A Masonic friend recommended him, an excellent teacher (trained in the University of Arizona before entering the seminary), to the superintendent of the Indian Agency at Sells, Arizona. He was hired. A few months later, he received a notice that he was accused of homosexuality and must disprove it within ten days or be fired.

He called me. The summer rains had delayed the mails. Five days of the deadline had passed. I urged him to come to Phoenix immediately to consult my attorney, a Mormon, and one of the best lawyers in the West.

His answer was one of futility. "How can you prove or disprove homosexuality—or why should you have to?"

My ex-priest friend lost his job. His grapevine informed him (ex-priests have them, too) that the archbishop of El Paso, Texas, where he had been stationed prior to his farewell to Rome, had contacted the archbishop of San Francisco, who was a member of the advisory committee of the U.S. Civil Service Commission of the region which covered Arizona. The dagger of the archbishop was as routine as burning at the stake in the good old days.

This ex-priest is now a Mason—as am I. He again works for the federal government. He has again been surveyed by the U.S. Civil Service Commission and has been confidentially told that every word of the story of his previous dismissal is true.

Many ex-priests have written me that they cannot get jobs with the government. Does the Catholic hierarchy control the American government?

The "shock troopers" of the hierarchy certainly do control the spiritual side of the Armed Forces of the United States.

As of mid-1959, all the Chiefs of Chaplains of the U.S. Army, U.S. Navy, and U.S. Air Force were Roman Catholic priests.

And these priests are so powerful in our alleged democracy that they can blackball out of the armed services any priest who dares defy Rome and quit the priesthood.

Father S. was a chaplain in the marines. He had gone through many landings in World War II against the Japanese.

After the war he, too, like thousands of priests, was disillusioned and quit Rome. He married and came to Phoenix to live. He told me his story.

He had been honorably discharged but was still in the reserves. He wished to transfer from the Chaplains Corps to the Intelligence Corps and go back into the service. He was rejected.

I wrote to Senator Barry Goldwater asking what an American citizen who had honorably served his country could do about further service.

The senator wrote the U.S. Navy. The U.S. Navy wrote the Roman Catholic Church and the Roman Catholic Church of the Archdiocese of New York said, "No!" So the U.S. Navy bowed in obedience to Rome; and Senator Barry Goldwater of Arizona humbly dismounted from the charger on which he stomps through the ranks of union labor, and bowed to Rome—as he has done before. And an ex-priest was blackballed. Here is the letter of the United States Navy. The letter insists this ex-chaplain "is a Catholic priest" even though he had definitely left the priesthood. The writer of this letter is a Catholic priest.

Department of the Navy
Bureau of Naval Personnel
Washington 25, D. C.

6 February 1953

My dear Senator Goldwater:

This is in reply to your letter of February 2, 1953, relative to the recommendation of the Chief of Chaplains concerning the application of Chaplain S., USNR, for a reclassification of his commission as that of a line officer.

Chaplain S. *is* a Catholic priest and it was not possible for the Chief of Chaplains to indicate to the Chief of Naval Personnel that his services should be utilized by the Navy Department in any other capacity than that of a clergyman.

On February 29, 1952, His Excellency, the Most Reverend James H. Griffiths, S.T.D., Auxiliary Bishop of the Archdiocese of New York and Chancellor of the Military Ordinariate, wrote to Chaplain S. W. Salisbury, USN, Chief of Chaplains of the U.S. Navy, and informed him that the ecclesiastical endorsement of Chaplain S. was on that date withdrawn. This action made it impossible for him to be ordered to the active Naval Service at any time. Accordingly, he was requested to submit his resignation from the Chaplain Corps of the Naval Reserve.

By direction of Chief of Naval Personnel:

Sincerely yours,

J. P. Mannion
Commander, CHC, USN
Assistant Director
Chaplains Division

Honorable Barry Goldwater
United States Senate
Washington, D. C.

There have been recent minor irritating acts of stupidity on the part of the U.S. military authorities in obeisance to Roman Catholic pressure, such as dedicating U.S. services to Catholic Saints. One service has been dedicated to St. Monica, another to St. Barbara, another to St. Christopher. These actions, of course, help nobody and hurt nobody and perhaps make some Catholic officers happy or make the chaplains think they are converting somebody to the "true faith."

For years there has been talk that the Roman Catholic Church controlled the United States State Department.

These are a few reasons for the apprehension among Protestants.

Immigrants are presumably not admitted into the

United States unless they are literate, able to support themselves and have been guaranteed jobs. I administer a hospital and have to give the U.S. Immigration Service these guarantees before I can get a foreign doctor into the country. I do this every year for the doctors we bring in.

Yet the news services constantly tell of nuns and priests being admitted in violation of the laws. They can't teach or preach or produce. I have personally seen them and tried to talk to them. All they could do was kneel and kiss the bishop's ring. Protestants and Other Americans United have repeatedly protested against these violations of American law.

A recent example is reported in *Church and State*, February, 1959. It indicates that nuns, particularly, are frequently admitted to the United States in evasion of the immigration regulations by special acts of Congress.

One Rep. Feighan, a co-religionist of Bishop Emmett M. Walsh of Youngstown, Ohio, introduced a special bill to admit for permanent residence Sister Mary Damion, Sister Maria Tarcisisia, and Sister Maria Regina, with the United States paying the visa fees.

The nuns are Italians—merely domestic servants, legally —normally not allowed to remain in the country; since they have no educational qualifications for preferential status under government quotas.

The bishop wanted to use these uneducated nuns as parochial school teachers. This bears out again the fact that Catholic schools need have no standards of teacher qualification. The bill for the admission of these nuns passed the House of Representatives.

In the days when I was studying for the priesthood (I

was ordained in 1933) the immigration regulations were undoubtedly different from those now in effect. But the importation of non-English-speaking priests to teach American children was as true then as now.

The Franciscan Orders' traditions in the West were Spanish and Mexican. California still boasts of the Camino Real (the Royal Highway)—the chain of Catholic missions reaching from San Diego to Sonoma, north of San Francisco, a tribute to the architectural genius and devotion of the Franciscan monks. They were actually built by the Indians, with some prodding by the Spanish soldiers.

The whole mission chain fell upon evil days with the independence of Mexico in 1833. No young monks came. The old ones died off. Santa Barbara became the only mission to maintain a continuity of religious service into the present century.

The spiritual care of the Indians and their civilization had gone by the board through all of California. The mission buildings themselves were mostly in ruins. Enthusiastic California history lovers made spasmodic attempts to preserve the buildings.

The Franco-Prussian War, with Bismarck rattling the sabre against the clergy, sent a swarm of German-Franciscan priests (deserting their flocks in their homeland) scurrying to the safety of America. They settled in the Middle West and were assigned to the "German National" churches in the German communities of many cities. They founded a "province" with junior and senior seminaries.

Some of them came west to care for the German-speaking immigrants. They took over the Santa Barbara Mission and in 1899 founded St. Anthony's Seminary in that city.

These native German priests, with accents thicker than the Irish priests who were staffing adjacent Irish parishes, recruited candidates for the priesthood from the children living in the areas they served.

The principal German parishes in California were St. Joseph's in Los Angeles, St. Boniface's and St. Anthony's in San Francisco, St. Elizabeth's in Oakland, and St. Francis in Sacramento.

When I entered the seminary in 1922, we still had priest-teachers who could hardly speak English. What, if any, educational qualifications they had, we never knew and some of them never demonstrated any. The priest-teachers who were native Americans were almost all of German parentage, brought up principally in the German ghettoes (and they were very real) of San Francisco.

We were being trained, in our final years of our twelve-year course, in "homiletics"—the science of religious preaching. Our teacher was a native-born imported German who spoke English with an intolerable accent. His knowledge of speaking English was deplorable.

My experience was not unusual. It is being widely repeated now, due to the wholesale importation of ignorant priests, brothers, and particularly nuns to fill the great shortage of parochial school teachers. The following is the observation of an ex-Catholic who has been a student of the Catholic "problem" for many years. These thoughts also point out an additional reason why very many Catholic children are transferred out of parochial schools and hence leave the Catholic Church:

Reasons why Catholic parents withdraw children from parochial schools:

1. Poor quality of education. This is especially true of the secondary schools. The grammar schools, which operate on a rote memory basis, manage to keep up quite well with the public schools, and actually surpass them in memory drill work. But the secondary schools, with their false and distorted version of history and literature, turn out graduates not merely ignorant but grossly misinformed. Any of these that go on to secular universities are at a tremendous disadvantage and often have to hire tutors and desperately cram to make matriculation requirements. In colleges giving entrance examinations, they invariably lose out.

2. Poor quality of teaching personnel. In most public school systems above the rural level, a B.A. degree is now required of teaching applicants. In addition, a heavy schedule of strictly professional courses must be pursued, and this continues throughout the teacher's teaching career. She is usually expected to go through a three-year probationary period before qualifying as a permanent teacher. She must, above all, be adept in child psychology. Catholic schools, on the other hand, due to the great dearth of "vocations" among young American Catholic women, have been reduced to bringing in peasant-type nuns from European countries. One Catholic mother, who put her sons in the public schools, told me recently that one of the Sisters in the parochial school they attended had defined grammar as "what learns you to speak correct." Other Sisters come into the class-room with heavy foreign accents which massacre the English language. Even of such Sisters there are not enough, and the Church is reduced to actually paying out "cash money"—an awful ordeal to the reverends and right reverends—as teachers' salaries to lay teachers. Since they pay the most miserable wage possible, one that wouldn't even hire a good garbage collector, they get a corresponding return. The teachers they can get for what they pay are mostly callow young girls or housewives whose children have grown or who don't happen to have any. Some times they are the type of devout unmarried Catholic lady who belongs to the

Third Order of St. Francis, makes the Nine Fridays regularly, and was a passionate supporter of Joe McCarthy. None of them have had any training in pedagogy, nor any successful experience with child psychology; and many have not even finished high school as far as their own educational attainments are concerned. Turn this type of teacher loose with the biased and lopsided Catholic curriculum which wastes about one-fourth of the time on prayers and church activities, and is it any wonder that intelligent Catholic parents are putting their children in the public schools?

Protestants and Other Americans United have also rightly objected to the State Department's connivance at the U.S. Catholic hierarchy's violation of the McCarran Act when the American cardinals went to Rome and voted for Pope John XXIII. To say that this vote of Spellman and McIntyre was purely a spiritual act and not connected with the act of civil government is not only a stupid lie but an insult to every intelligent American.

The complete revelation of the State Department's submission to the "shock troopers" came to me in a conference with Mrs. Pearl Mesta, known for years as the "hostess with the mostest."

She had been the U.S. Ambassador to Luxemburg. I had heard for many years that the Roman hierarchy controlled the United States State Department. Many Protestants have been concerned because the only school for foreign service was at Georgetown University in Washington, a Jesuit school. This guaranteed that the bulk of our consular employees around the world would be Catholics or at least exposed to Jesuit indoctrination.

The success of Senator Joe McCarthy in expurgating the overseas American libraries of books he considered subversive points up the Roman Catholic control.

Mrs. Mesta told me that, while she was Ambassador to Luxemburg, Eleanor Roosevelt arranged for an official visit to the country. She, Mrs. Mesta, received orders from the American Embassy in Rome that Mrs. Mesta was to have Mrs. Roosevelt's picture taken with the abbot of a famous monastery and be interviewed with him by the press. The story and the pictures were to be released to the news services for transmission around the world.

Mrs. Mesta told me that she and Mrs. Roosevelt sat up most of the night discussing the insidious increasing inroads of the Roman Catholic Church into the agencies of the Federal Government of the United States.

I asked her the blunt question, "Does the Roman Catholic Church control the U.S. State Department?" "Yes," she said, "around the world."

Only recently the Methodists established a School of Foreign Service in their American University to try to checkmate the Jesuits at Georgetown.

To learn the extent of the infiltration of Roman Catholic "shock troopers" into the state governments of the Union would require an army of investigators and sleuths. We know that many states have Catholic governors. We know that the wishes of Protestant majorities are snubbed by Catholic controlling interests in some state legislatures.

The outstanding example of the hierarchy's ruthless ramrodding technique, when it has the power to exercise it through its parochial-school-trained serfs, concerns the question of birth control.

The hierarchy, all of whom claim to be Americans and in favor of the freedoms guaranteed by the Constitution, keep the pressure on the legislatures of some eastern states, to prevent the relaxing of laws forbidding doctors, druggists, and clinics from dispensing birth control information, and selling appliances even to Protestants.

This is one of the most serious and intricate examples of Roman Catholic control of America by "shock troopers." Fortunately, the bishops are strong enough now in only a few Church-controlled New England states like Massachusetts and Rhode Island to enforce their medically, socially, and economically tyrannical will on all the people. But this is an example of the local states' bishops' sincere feeling that they are by divine prerogative the super states to keep the civil governments in line when they have the legislative power to do it.

The rights of a dissenting Protestant minority mean nothing to them. They are the "Princes" of the Church and as such the authority of God Himself.

I can well remember Bishop Daniel J. Gercke, whose authority covers most of Arizona, and whose confessions I heard many times, bragging about being a prince of the Church and stating that that position made him the equivalent in authority of one of the twelve apostles of Christ.

One of the obvious violations of the principle of separation of church and state that the bishops have rammed through many state legislatures is the provision of state tax funds for bus transportation for parochial school children. The Jesuit priest, Virgil Blum of Loyola University, has employed in Catholic press articles the normal Jesuit twist of accusing Protestants of persecuting Catholics by denying not only bus transportation but complete subsidy to Catholic children in Catholic schools. The pattern of

Quebec, Holland, and Belgium is now the norm for America, according to him.

In all of the maneuvers in state legislatures, the "shock troopers," the graduates of the parochial school system, are the yeomen who do the work and carry out the orders of the hierarchy.

One situation that could well be examined by concerned Protestant groups in every state is the relationship between state legislatures and superior courts and the handling of juvenile delinquents in the states. Associated with juvenile delinquency is the pattern of the adoption of babies.

In my sovereign state of Arizona, the only institution in the state for the commitment of delinquent girls is the Roman Catholic "Good Shepherds Convent." The superior court judges send the girls there. The state taxpayers pay the bills. The nuns don't want pregnant girls so they have to send them out of the state or to a Florence Crittenton Home.

Within a few years, the nuns have built an imposing plant, presumably at the taxpayers' expense for the proselytizing of Protestant girls in distress. A Catholic chaplain, a Jesuit, is always available to the girls. Protestant chaplains are sometimes admitted, but many times refused on the grounds that the girls have adequate spiritual advice.

The poor girls are virtual peons, and must work in the laundry, kitchen, and other departments, even though we taxpayers are paying the nuns to reform these youngsters.

The following report in 1958 is from an agency of the U.S. Government, the National Probation and Parole Association.

Several interesting angles came out in the report. One

was that half of the girls were Catholic—in a state with a population not more than twenty per cent Catholic. Most of the magazines in the library were Catholic:

> In spite of these deliberate efforts to create a more non-sectarian atmosphere in the school, its program, nevertheless, is based upon a system of religious beliefs and practices to which all of the girls are exposed.
>
> It is recommended that the state build a training school for girls to care for the non-Catholic girls and those Catholic girls who do not respond to the Good Shepherd program.

It would be very interesting to know how many other states have had similar experiences with Catholic Good Shepherd convents for girls.

To what extent the parochial school system graduates have taken over county government in America would require a very detailed and extensive study. It would have to cover employment policies in all county departments, including particularly the sheriffs' offices, county attorneys' offices and county hospital policies.

A situation that has developed in our county, Maricopa, illustrates the point that the hierarchy does not need great numbers to achieve its aims. Sometimes a very small number of dedicated "shock troopers" or easily susceptible Catholics can quietly do the work. The Medical Director of the Maricopa County Health Department issued orders to all county nurses (July, 1959) that they are forbidden to give birth control information in any conferences in clinics or in home visits. Nor may they refer inquiring mothers to clinics, such as ours, where they can get the information. An overwhelming majority of this county are Protestants. The bulk of the taxes paying the nurses' salaries are from non-Catholics.

There are three members of the Board of Supervisors. Two are Catholic. The county manager is a Catholic. The clergy, through only three people, can ram Roman Catholic law down the throats of an entire county of a half million people. This is a sample, and it is being duplicated in many other cities and counties, of what I mean by saying that the dedication of only a fourth of parochial school pupils can and is destroying our freedom.

Roman Catholic (usually Irish or Italian) control of major city politics in America has been so disgracefully bad for so long that, if the Soviet knew it, they would be sure that we are on the verge of self-annihilation by national default.

The Roman Catholic corruption of Curley in Boston, Jimmy Walker and O'Dwyer in New York, Hague in New Jersey, Pendergast in Kansas City, is so notorious that people take it for granted.

It has been repeated over and over again in cities across the country. It is a tremendous tribute to the strength of the Protestant and Jewish stability that our society has survived. The strange code of ethics that I found in Phoenix years ago was that prostitution must be condoned, other crimes must be glossed over, if the "super-proper" citizens contributed enough to the Church and the amenities were taken care of.

With this happening in a nominally Protestant city, it is not difficult to picture the Catholic control in San Francisco, Milwaukee, Chicago, Pittsburgh, New Orleans or Boston, or any number of other American cities that have been admittedly sucked into the orbit of Roman

Catholic (usually Irish, Polish or Italian) political and moral control.

The "moral" control is usually an anomaly because it means only the control of things the Catholic hierarchy does not like. Again this power is exercised by the hierarchy through the devoted percentage who will vote right and be responsive when they are elected.

In July, 1959, the city aldermen in Nashua, New Hampshire, voted unanimously to sell the Lake St. Public School to St. Joseph's Catholic Church for one thousand dollars.

In New York City, the authorities agreed to sell a very substantial part of land condemned for an Urban Redevelopment Program (a later development of the old slum clearance programs) to the Jesuit Fordham University for a fraction of its true value.

The Jesuits maneuvered the same arrangement of almost "donated" valuable city land out of the subservient powers in St. Louis, Missouri. This was to be used for their St. Louis University, again out of Urban Redevelopment property. The Protestants of Missouri have been fighting this city "give-away" very vigorously.

Lay Catholics and priests frequently try to tell non-Catholics that the hierarchy does not enter into politics and does not try to tell the faithful how to vote in either local or national elections. This is simply not true. Whenever it is to the advantage of the Church, it is in politics up to its ears. In a recent issue in Missouri over public bus transportation for Catholic school children, the bishops of the state sent vigorous telegrams to all legislators threatening to get them in the next election if they didn't vote right on the issue. The same un-American maneuver was used by the bishops of Rhode Island when there was a move to abolish the state's law on birth control information. Then the bishops argue that the "people" want the law.

As I have lectured across the country, people in many cities have told me how local priests have condemned public school bond issues from the pulpit and have defeated them. This happened in September, 1958, in the school district in which I live. The Catholic pastor was pressuring his people for funds and pledges to pay for their elaborate new church. The public school district was so overcrowded that over a thousand children were subjected to double sessions. The priest didn't care. He told his people at Sunday Mass that they were burdened enough with their own school and new church and should not be double taxed. He recommended that they vote against the bond issue. They did and it was defeated. This type of control in school elections is easy for the clergy to accomplish with only a few devoted "shock troopers," because only a handful of citizens show any interest in the school system and its election.

The "shock trooper" fronts cover many other fields than those of national, state, county, or local politics.

One is labor . . .

The historic Catholic tie-in with organized labor is undoubtedly due to the fact that most Catholic immigrants were unskilled laborers and perforce relied on the unions for survival.

The smartest among them saw the opportunities of less work and more money by becoming officials of the unions. The rest of the movement is history.

The past president of the A.F.L. was a Catholic, William Green. Phillip Murray, the late president of the C.I.O., was a Catholic. George Meany, the current president of the AFL-CIO, is a Roman Catholic. The leaders of many other national unions are Roman Catholics.

I know most of the leaders of the union movement in Central Arizona. The majority of them are Protestants. Many of them have been in their unions for many years, are acquainted with national labor leaders, and have been delegates to the national conventions.

I asked one of them, "How many of the national offices (they are usually called "international") of labor unions are run by Roman Catholics?"

His answer, "Practically all of them!"

This is a field in which the "storm troopers" have certainly been successfully busy.

Our hospital is one of the first in America to voluntarily become a union institution. Our hospital cafeteria is probably the only one, or one of the very few, in America to display the sign, "This is a Union House."

In token of this cooperation or collaboration, I was presented with a life time honorary membership in the Hotel & Restaurant Employees and Bartenders International Union A.F.L., No. 631.

Of my union membership and our hospital's almost unique happy relationship with organized labor, I am intensely proud. The chairman of our board of trustees is the business agent of the Operating Engineers, William Gray.

Other members are the secretary of the Carpenters Union, John McNeill; the business agent of the Painters Union, Bancroft Nolan; the editor of the Arizona LABOR JOURNAL, Ralph Sprague. Another is Elmer Vickers, a retired executive of the AFL-CIO of Arizona.

But the union of which I am a member is apparently controlled by the Roman Catholic Church. One entertainer, Danny Thomas, picked up the torch for a Roman Catholic St. Jude's Hospital in Kentucky. The International Union voted many thousands of dollars for this Catholic hospital. Local union members were strongly urged to make similar contributions.

There are also the Catholic Trade Union groups drawing people from many different unions. The purpose here again is to keep them actively tied to the hierarchy and to train them to go back to their individual unions and work to preserve the "rights of the church." This is not too difficult to do. Many unions with over a thousand members have attendance at meetings of only a few dozen. It is a simple matter for a mere handful of dedicated Catholic members to ram through Catholic officers or business agents without the membership at large even knowing what has happened. Again the hierarchy does not need great numbers.

A field in which "shock troopers" are not only being trained but are quietly doing effective work for the Holy Mother Church is in nursing. I told, in describing my own ministry, of my work in teaching student nurses in the Catholic system of hospital and medical ethics. The same is taught in Catholic Nursing Schools across the country.

This may strike the average non-Catholic as a rather insignificant influence on the American scene. But there are almost a thousand sisters' hospitals in the country. Very many of them have nursing schools. They train approximately one-third of all the registered nurses in

America—a very great percentage, probably half of them non-Catholic. But all of these girls are trained in the Roman Catholic code of medical ethics—no abortions, or any other procedure that might directly terminate the life of the fetus, no contraception, the baptism of all babies in danger of death, regardless of the wishes of the parents. These Catholic nursing graduates go everywhere and take the practice of Catholic ethics into almost every hospital in America. When we realize that hospitals constitute one of the largest industries in America, handling over twenty-three million patients per year, we can see what a clever and far reaching maneuver this dream of the "shock troopers" can be.

Earlier, I have cited Church censorship as a planned diet designed to stunt the ken of parochial school students. Too much cannot be said about this subject. It is a gangrene that eats at the bones and muscles of our citizenry. Roman Catholic censorship in America is one of the most flagrant and vicious violations of the American principle of freedom of speech, with its necessary corollaries of freedom of thought and freedom of writing. The various forms of censorship are not yet as effective as the hierarchy would wish; but they are painfully apparent in communities across the country.

This censorship is intended to control both Protestants and Catholics, or it would not be exercised in the manner it is. It is intended to keep the devout mentally in line and to increase their loyalty.

The area of censorship also enables the hierarchy to make use of a very large number of lay "shock troopers";

and intelligence need not be their outstanding characteristic for this type of work.

The Church has established a censorship agency "CARTA"—the Catholic Association for Radio, Television, and Advertising. It extends beyond these media and also includes the press. The new Pope has strongly stressed the tremendous importance of the hierarchy's watchfulness over means of communication and entertainment.

The censorship over the nation's press is largely a silent, unexpressed control. Editors know from the experience of a few rash papers how swift, cruel and un-American a bishop's boycott can be. Almost never do the papers carry news items about the aberrations of priests, such as drunk and reckless driving, or having accidents while having a parishioner's wife in the car. The San Francisco NEWS printed such an item some years ago. The archbishop had a "pastoral" letter read in all churches the next Sunday denouncing the paper as anti-Catholic and demanding that Catholics cancel their subscriptions. The paper lost several thousand subscribers.

In the spring of 1959, an incident happened in Hawaii that normally would have hit the news wires. A local priest's clothing was found on one of the beaches. He was presumed dead and a requiem mass was said by the pastor. A few days later a local paper in Honolulu discovered that, instead of drowning, the priest had flown by United Airlines to California, where he met the lady secretary from his parish in Hawaii. The taxi driver who had revealed that he took the priest to the airport was warned to "keep his mouth shut" for the sake of his own family. As far as I could find out, this interesting story did not appear in any mainland papers.

In many cities where I have lectured, including Los Angeles, but especially in New England, newspapers have been afraid to accept paid advertisements of my appearances. Even in Phoenix, the Arizona REPUBLIC and Phoenix GAZETTE refused to accept the paid advertisement unless the title of my lecture, which contained a reference to the Catholic Church, was omitted. The New York TIMES refused to print any review of my book, even though it was a best seller for five years.

Fortunately, there are some papers in the country that refuse to be browbeaten by the local priests and bishops and print the truth without fear.

The story of magazines is the same as that of newspapers, except that the threat of pressure is generally through the advertisers.

The censorship of books is the oldest weapon of the hierarchy in its attempt to control men's minds. The infamous *Index of Forbidden Books* has been mentioned in detail earlier. It might be well to emphasize, though, that a book need not be listed by name to be forbidden. Whole categories of books are damned, such as books like this that are critical of the Church. This enables bishops and even priests to catch books as they come off the press and warn the devout.

The devout or the "shock troopers" seem to be the only ones who pay any attention to the *Index*. My book, *People's Padre*, has been condemned for several years. Yet very many Catholics, including students, have read it. They have written me from all over the country; and many in Phoenix have called me with questions on parts that puzzled them. One boy from St. Mary's High School told me that a group in his class were reading it and preparing lists of questions from it which they were asking the priests in the classroom.

With many American publishing houses, the mere fear of Church condemnation prevents them from accepting a critical manuscript. Mine was rejected by four major New York firms for this reason. An editor of one of New York's most successful houses told me that the owner was violently opposed to the Catholic Church, principally because of censorship, but he didn't dare publish anything critical because he might lose his very lucrative Catholic school textbook business.

This editor also told me that the customary procedure is to publish these textbooks for public schools. Copies are sent to Catholic school authorities, who delete objectionable passages or chapters, substitute their own pro-Catholic material, and the book is republished with the hierarchy's approbation.

To me the classic way of evading the Church's law was contained in a letter from a Catholic woman, who criticized my book severely. She wrote that she wasn't permitted to read it, but had a Protestant neighbor read it to her.

Another "shock trooper" method of controlling reading is through the Catholic public librarians. Their technique is to buy as many Catholic books and magazines as possible, push them on the public and keep all critical books in the background or in the locked compartments, presumably for safekeeping. I have had letters from many

The hierarchy's most effective control of books before smaller communities saying that their Catholic public librarians refused to order my book on the grounds that it is not up to the literary standards of the town.

they are published is in the paperback field through the National Organization for Decent Literature. In a previous chapter, I explained how this organization utilized the "shock troopers" and even school children in boycotts of stores selling books objectionable to them in the city of Pittsburgh.

This movement, again utilizing only a relatively few people, scares the publishers who see the ogre of thirty to forty million customers boycotting their books. They either cut down the size of the printing of certain titles or don't publish them at all. County pharmaceutical societies recommend to their drugstores the elimination of titles the Church objects to. Under this pressure a New York pharmacists' association agreed to remove five hundred different comic books, periodicals and paperbacks.

Thus the Catholic Church is deliberately and effectively censoring and regimenting the reading materials of all Americans, not just Catholics. It is impossible to reconcile this mental tyranny with the clergy's (and Senator John Kennedy's) statements that they endorse and practice the fundamental American principles of freedom of thought and freedom of speech.

When the N.O.D.L. is called to account on this violation of American liberty, its reply is that it condemns only obscene books and certainly all America must agree on their elimination. The obvious answer is that the rest of America has the right to make its own decision as to what it considers obscene.

Among the condemned books are countless outstanding literary works, many of which have been acclaimed for years.

Roman Catholic censorship of movies has been long-standing, through the Legion of Decency. This organization issues periodical classifications of motion pictures with "condemned" covering those that the faithful are forbidden to see. These lists are published in Catholic weeklies. However, as in the situation of paperback books, the hierarchy prefers to control the films at their source or before they are made. For many years it controlled the Production Code Administration, which for years was called the "Breen Office" because a responsive Catholic named Breen was its executive. Members of the clergy are on tap to assist in protecting the Church's position and rights. This watch dog attitude is undoubtedly the reason the studios are so unrealistically gentle in their treatment of the Roman Church. They make moral heroes of the priests, sell sacrificing angels of the nuns and portray the Church as a gentle kindly mother to mankind. Fortunately, in recent years the studios have rebelled repeatedly at this iron hand and lawsuits which have reached the Supreme Court have at least partially broken the power of state Catholic censorship groups.

However, the clergy still uses the boycott methods on local theatres. Here the army of the shock troopers is mustered. Sometimes the bishop will order a theatre boycotted for months (regardless of the pictures it is showing) if it has shown a film objectionable to the episcopal nostrils. Sometimes the faithful man a picket line. Sometimes, if the devout are numerous enough, the bishop decides to break a theatre. The following is an example of how he can succeed. This was reported in *Church and State* (December, 1958).

In Lake Placid, New York, the local priest, Fr. James

T. Lyng, ordered the non-Catholic manager of the Palace Theatre not to show a Brigitte Bardot film, "The Bride Is Much Too Beautiful." The manager refused to obey the priest. The priest ordered a six months' boycott, regardless of the pictures. The theatre, the only one in the community, went broke. Protestant Americans were deprived of all motion pictures because the Catholic Church objected to one picture. The frightening thing again is this: If the hierarchy has this power when it is in its present minority and dares to ruthlessly exercise it now, what will it (especially some of its more ignorant and arrogant Irish priests and bishops) do, if and when it achieves a numerical or alleged numerical majority?

The self-appointed guardians of everybody's morality have not overlooked television. Since so many programs are filmed, they can nip these at the source in Hollywood. As with the control of magazines, in TV, too, the method of control can be the threat of pressure on the sponsor. Certainly, the manufacturer of soap, lipstick, or peanut butter would not want thirty million potential customers told by their leaders not to buy their products because the film is anti-Catholic. As a result, we see in a Western the historically anachronous situation of a Franciscan monk fighting for righteousness and the underdog in a bar of a frontier town in Dodge City or wild section of Oklahoma. The early Franciscan monks didn't know those spots existed.

An additional technique in television is telephone pressure. Since TV schedules are published far in advance, the clergy can get word out to the "shock troopers," who can line up enough others to lay down a telephone barrage on a station manager protesting an offending program.

This happened in Chicago after the film, "Martin Luther," was scheduled. Most Catholics had not even seen the film; but the priests said it was "historically unacceptable" to Catholics and that was enough.

The same situation happened in Washington, D. C., when WTOP-TV, owned by the Washington POST refused to show "Martin Luther" because of Roman Catholic pressure.

A rather frightening point to consider is that this cultural sterilization is not something that we apprehensive, experienced ex-Catholics are gloomily forecasting for the future when the Catholic Church shall have achieved a majority in this nation. This is a sort of an advance flexing of the hierarchical muscles. This blight is very much in effect and is spreading over the nation now, when the Church claims only about eighteen per cent of the population. This is merely a mild foretaste of what we can expect if the Church ever gets fifty-one per cent of the nation.

CHAPTER THIRTEEN

Shock Troop Assault
on American Public Schools

To those who are students of the Roman Church's non-religious activities in America, the unpublicized but steady movement to control education is by far the most serious present threat to American freedom and institutions.

Popes have claimed in their encyclicals that the Roman Church has been designated by Christ as the Mother of Learning and Education throughout the world for all people. Previous chapters have told the story of the Catholic School, its failures, its successes, and its attempted un-American indoctrination of over four million American children in the suppression of freedom of thought.

This system is expanding so rapidly that the hierarchy is sore put to keep up financially with the expansion of buildings or the payment of teachers.

The ultimate aim is financial support from the U.S. Government, and later the states also, for the Catholic school system. At the present time, the "shock troopers" in the parochial schools are being conditioned by the Catholic press for their future work in writing to congress-

men when appropriate bills for the relief of the hierarchy
are introduced.

The strategy of this campaign is being handled by the
Jesuits. Not only are they thoroughly capable of this type
of connivance but, with their chain of colleges and universities, they have a tremendous financial investment at
stake.

The development of the build-up of argument is a
masterpiece of Jesuit reasoning—or the appearance of
reasoning. Watch it!

When I was a youngster, the Catholic schools were
happy to pick up some discarded textbooks from the
public schools.

During the depression, our government started giving
surplus food to schools so that children might have at
least one warm meal a day. Catholic schools were included.

As public schools began to furnish bus service to students in some states, Catholic schools were again included. When some citizens objected, on the grounds that
this violated the principle of separation of church and
state, laws were passed in a few states permitting the
practice.

States which now supply public money for parochial
school children to ride on buses are: California, Indiana,
Kentucky, Louisiana, Massachusetts, Michigan, New
Hampshire, New Jersey, New Mexico, New York, Illinois,
Kansas, Oregon, Rhode Island, and Connecticut.

This free bus transportation is no longer regarded as
a privilege by the hierarchy, but rather as a *right*. In
1955, the annual statement of the bishops' conference
included these words: "The students of these parochial

schools have the right to benefit from those measures, grants, or aid, which are manifestly designed for the health, safety, and welfare of American youth, irrespective of the school attended." The word "welfare" disclosed one step of the strategy of the Jesuits in taking the whole matter of bus transportation out of the school system and putting it in the welfare department. The denial of this welfare then is pictured as an act of cruelty on the part of the various states, or even as a violation of the Constitution. The Reverend Virgil Blum, a Jesuit, is quoted in Catholic papers as follows: "If the state government deprives Catholic children of the right to share in the benefits of welfare legislation; for example, of bus transportation because they go to a parochial school, the government violates their religious liberty. Depriving these children of bus transportation moreover violates the right under the 14th Amendment to share equally in welfare benefits."

The plot unfolds. Welfare. The government is obligated to provide welfare benefits to Catholic children. The toilets of a school are not directly educational. They serve the welfare needs of students. So do the walls, the roof, and the desks.

Jesuit Blum has gone further in his recent reasoning. Protestants who have fought the financial encroachments of the hierarchy have done so on the grounds that public support of parochial schools would be a violation of the First Amendment—a violation of the principle of separation of church and state. Senator John Kennedy made a public statement concurring in this viewpoint and was condemned by the Catholic press. Protestants certainly agree that any church may have schools and American children may attend any of them; but it is important to note that the government is not permitted to support them.

Jesuit Blum has now evolved his logic to the point where he contends that, if the U. S. Government does not support parochial schools, it is illegally *persecuting* Catholic children because they practice their religion. (*U. S. News and World Report*, October 25, 1957.)

The largest and most far reaching program that the Catholic school trained "shock troopers" are now becoming increasingly engaged in is the control of the public schools of America—I repeat—the control of the public schools of America.

This movement is still relatively recent. Many people have not even heard that it is going on. But it certainly is. It is the most serious threat to our democracy and its free institutions that could be conceived. The public school is certainly the sanctuary of democracy, the Holy of Holies of our most sacred principles, and the most effective channel of passing on the ideals of Washington, Jefferson, Franklin, and Lincoln from generation to generation. And yet a power-hungry hierarchy, through a relative handful of dedicated zealots, most of whom are parochial school graduates, can take the greatest part of this system away from the public—unless it wakes up.

A natural question arises. Why should the Catholic Church want control of the public schools? For years it has condemned them publicly and in its "trade" magazines for priests as godless, materialistic, immoral centers. Canon Law #1374 forbids Catholic children to attend them. In some American dioceses, parents can be refused absolution if they send their children to public schools.

There are many reasons, however, why the hierarchy wants this control. It claims that its own school system is able to accommodate only about half the Catholic children of the country. Many parents won't send their youngsters to parochial schools because of their inferior quality. Catholic teachers in public schools can keep track of Catholic children, remind them of Sunday Mass and encourage them to attend Catholic social affairs. Catholic teachers can and do refuse to discuss subjects in class, historical or otherwise, that are embarrassing or offensive to the Catholic Church. The following letter from New Ulm, Minnesota, is an example:

Dear Sir:
Several of the members of my senior class at New Ulm High School have read your book, *People's Padre*. Our college prep teacher feels she shouldn't allow us to give an oral book report on your book in class. The reason she gives is that you have been proven insane. (She is Catholic.) We would like to know if you have been retained as superintendent of Memorial Hospital. We feel that would be ample proof of your sanity. As our school is a public school, we feel this is an issue of free speech, and she has no right to refuse unless you are insane, and that still wouldn't make much difference to me. I hope we don't inconvenience you too much.

When Catholics control a school board, they can also control the textbooks. This applies particularly to history books which may tell the true story of the Church's history. They are afraid that facts of the Inquisition, spreading over four centuries of torture and murder of nonconforming Christians, apostates and witches might shock the young Catholic students right out of the Church.

The Church achieves control of public schools in two

ways: by placing a majority of Catholic "shock troopers" on school boards and by infiltrating the schools with Catholic teachers.

It would probably take a personal trip to catalogue all the areas, urban and suburban, where the Church has already taken over the school boards. On my lecture tours I found it to be true in many cities. In Boston, the situation is so flagrant that the school board has taken it upon itself to sell to the archbishop about a dozen public plants for a mere token sum. They were to be converted into parochial schools.

Throughout New England, the people, some Protestant minority school board members, told me that the great majority of boards were controlled by Catholics and most of the teachers were Catholics.

In a large Massachusetts city, a teacher told me that one Protestant and one Jewish teacher were hired in the high school to give the semblance of fairness. All other teachers were Catholics. In a nearby normal school, another teacher reported, eighty percent of the students were Catholics. In Chicago I was told that seventy percent of public school teachers are Catholics, while in New Orleans it is said to be ninety percent. Even if some of these figures are exaggerated, the responsible Protestant leaders in all these cities know that Catholic teachers are in the great majority. I did not receive this information from the man in the street, but from teachers and the leaders of the local ministerial associations.

In one New England city, I was told by a public school teacher that what irked her particularly was the voice of Archbishop (now Cardinal) Cushing coming through the loud speaker in the morning reciting the Rosary—in a public school. Another teacher told me of the statue of the Virgin Mary on a pedestal in a neighboring class room in a public school taught by a Catholic teacher.

This actual Catholic control does not exist only in New England. When I spoke in Erie, Pennsylvania, I was informed that all five members of the school board were Catholic. When I was in Gary, Indiana, a prominent minister told me that the mayor was a Catholic. He had authority to appoint the school board; so a majority was Catholic.

In Marion County in Kentucky, the battle has been raging for years between Protestants and the Catholic school board who are trying to force Protestant children to attend a Catholic high school, taught by nuns, which the board is subsidizing as a public school.

Many people write to me from various parts of the country talking about this issue and saying, as though it happened nowhere else, that "we here are under control of the Catholic Church." These letters come from all parts of the United States.

One instance that recently occurred is in the presumably Protestant state of Texas. The city is Bremond, Texas. The school in question is St. Mary's Elementary School. It has been leased to the public school district for one dollar a year. The school is staffed by nuns, who teach in the garb of their Order. Their salaries are paid from public funds and turned over to the Roman Catholic Church. Incidentally, by a rule of Internal Revenue Department, nuns teaching in public schools do not have to pay withholding taxes. They turn the amount in full over to their religious order. This does not apply to Baptists, Methodists, or other teachers in public schools. In this particular school, crucifixes and religious pictures, the symbols of the Roman Catholic Church, hang on the walls of what is supposedly a public school.

At the present time a lawsuit is in progress against the school board. It was initiated by a Methodist pastor, Earl McIntyre. He contends, "The school is, in fact, a parochial school, receiving state aid in violation of the law."

In New Mexico, most of the school boards are under the control of Catholics.

Protestants and Other Americans United report that in twenty-one states nuns are on the public payroll, teaching in two hundred and eighty-one public schools. Two thousand and fifty-five Roman nuns, brothers, and priests are teaching in the public schools of the United States. In the city of Sterling in Logan County, Colorado, the hierarchy went so far, when it gained control of the school board, as to abolish the public school and then named St. Peter's Catholic School as the public school of the area. It fired the public school teachers and put the nuns on the payroll. It was only through the alertness of the County Treasurer, who was a 32nd Degree Mason, that this case went to court and the public school was finally restored to the public. This same County Treasurer told me that there are still many so-called public schools in Colorado in which nuns are teaching. These areas show again the control of the clergy.

There is certainly a field in this matter for a special study as to the exact extent of Catholic board and teacher control in the thousands of public schools across the country. I have merely touched on the problem.

These facts are frightening enough to sincere thoughtful Americans. The natural question is: How did the hierarchy get control of these school boards? The answer is simple. Only a very small percentage of voters turn out for school elections. I live in a school district of some thirty thousand people. At school elections only a couple of hundred vote. This disgraceful neglect is true even in school bond elections involving millions of dollars.

I have tried to touch on the results achieved by the Church in her indoctrination through the parochial school system, even though that training secured the self-sacrificing devotion of only a minority of the children who are exposed to it. It is not a pleasant picture to those of us who love America and its freedoms.

At this time, when there is the possibility of a Catholic president of the United States, we hear much of tolerance. Tolerance is a virtue—if no one is being hurt because of it. But it is criminal if it is merely a word covering laziness, cowardice, ignorance, or indifference to the welfare of the nation and its freedoms.

Many non-Catholic Americans act as though freedom of thought, of speech and of worship have been with us forever and will last forever.

Contemporary history should violently teach us otherwise. So should also the dust of other countries.

In the past, republics and democracies have died while their citizens talked and played and were tolerant. The greatest of these was probably that of early Rome. Its freedoms were destroyed by an Emperor and by a rising dictatorial Church. But the masses of its citizens did not recognize the rape of their democracy. Their leaders told them that they were free. As Romans, they gloated over foreign gladiators who fought each other and challenged the lions in the great coliseums. They proudly saluted the symbol of their freedom—the banner with the letters S P Q R—*Senatus Populusque Romanus*— (The Senate and the Roman People)—while all the time their senate was dead and the Roman people were mental slaves.

May God grant that American citizenship may never become a mere mockery of freedom and that our people may never trade their principles for a flag and their birthright for "bread and circuses."

Notes

All quotations from the Popes in this book, unless otherwise noted, are from the *Enchiridion*. The full title of the book is *Enchiridion Symbolorum Definitionum et Declarationum de Rebus Fidei et Murum—The Compilation of Decrees, Definitions and Declarations on Matters of Faith and Morals*. It contains the core of the decrees from Clement I in the year 90 A.D. to pronouncements of Pius XII in November, 1950 A.D. It was originally compiled in 1854 by a Jesuit, one Henry Denzinger. The quotations here are from the 28th edition, published in Barcelona, Spain, by the Herder Book Company, in 1952. It carries the official "Nihil Obstat" and "Imprimatur."

I. *The Well-Washed Brain*

1. Enchiridion Symbolorum. P. 641, Enc. "Divini" Illius Magistri, Dec. 31, 1929

2. Pfeffer, Leo. Church, State, and Freedom. Boston, Beacon Press, 1953, p. 425.

3. Philosophy of the curriculum of the Catholic elementary school. Washington, D.C., Catholic University of America Press, 1954, p. 38.

4. *Ibid.* P. 87.

5. *Ibid.* P. 138.

6. *Ibid.* P. 71.

II. *Education by Edict*

1. Hartnett, R. C. (S. J.). Equal rights for children. N. Y., America Press, pp. 32-33.

2. Catholic school guide. N. Y., Catholic News, 1954, p. 3.

3. Pfeffer, Leo. Church, State, and Freedom. P. 427.

III. *The Three S's—Sex, Sin and Satan*

1. Baltimore catechism. N. Y., Benziger Brothers, p. 64.

2. Jone, Heribert. Moral theology. Westminster, Md., Newman Press, 1952, p. 146.

3. Baltimore catechism. P. 168.

4. Jone, Heribert. Moral theology. P. 217.
Noldin, Jerome. Summa theologiae moralis. Westminster, Md., Newman Press, 1952, Vol. II, p. 378 seq.
Davis, Henry (S. J.). A summary of moral and pastoral theology. N. Y., Sheed and Ward, 1952, pp. 88-89.

5. Davis, Henry (S. J.). A summary of moral and pastoral theology. P. 114.
Jone, Heribert. Moral theology. P. 248.
Noldin, Jerome. Summa theologiae moralis. P. 555.

6. Jone, Heribert. Moral theology. P. 249.
Davis, Henry (S. J.). A summary of moral and pastoral theology. P. 115.
Noldin, Jerome. Summa theologiae moralis. P. 557.

IV. *The Mystique*

1. Ritual romanum. N. Y., Benziger Brothers, 1947, pp. 375-578.

2. Fromm, Erich. Psychoanalysis and religion. New Haven, Yale University Press, 1950, pp. 109-111.

3. Sullivan, William L. Under orders. N. Y., Richard Smith, 1945, p. 36.

4. How our nation began. N. Y., William H. Sadlier, Inc., 1954. Imprimatur Francis Cardinal Spellman.

VI. *Censorship in the Textbooks*

1. Durant, Will. The age of faith. N. Y., Simon and Schuster, 1950, p. 774, 779.

2. Lea, Henry Charles. History of the inquisition of the Middle Ages. N. Y., Russell & Russell, Vol. I, pp. 337-367.

3. *Ibid.*, Vol. I., P. 550.

4. Durant, Will. The age of faith. P. 783.

5. *Ibid.* P. 784.

6. Encyl. Britt. v. Salem.

7. Lea, Henry Charles. History of the inquisition of the Middle Ages. Vol. III, p. 549.

8. Pontificale Romanum Summorum Pontificum (The Roman Pontifical of the Supreme Pontiffs). Issued by Sacred Congregation of Rites, approved by Cardinal Van Roey, March 3, 1934, H. Dessain, Publishers to the Supreme Pontiff, and the Congregation of Rites and the Propagation of the Faith, p. 133.

9. Enchiridion Symbolorum. P. 447.

10. *Ibid.* P. 533.

11. Pontificale Romanum Summorum Pontificum. Belgium, Mechlin, p. 133.

12. Enchiridion Symbolorum. P. 488.

13. *Ibid.* P. 562.

14. *Time* Magazine, November 15, 1954, p. 59.

15. Arizona CATHOLIC REGISTER, March 11, 1955.

16. Enchiridion Symbolorum. P. 219.

17. *Ibid.* P. 386.

VII. *The Malignancy of Censorship*

1. Sugrue, Thomas. A Catholic speaks his mind. N. Y., Harper & Brothers, pp. 5-7.

IX. *The Critics Speak from Many Vantages*

1. Moehlman, Conrad. School and church: The American way. N. Y., Harper & Brothers, 1944, p. 78.

2. Cunneen, J. E. Catholicism in America. N. Y., Harcourt, Brace and Co., 1947, p. 144.

3. *Ibid*. P. 156.

4. *Ibid*. P. 149.

5. *Ibid*. P. 169 seq.

6. *Ibid*. P. 183.

7. *Ibid*. P. 188.

8. The Social Structure of American Catholics, by John Kane, University of Notre Dame—presented at the convention of the American Catholic Sociological Society—Loyola University (Jesuit)—January, 1955.

9. *Ibid*. Pp. 3-4.

10. *Ibid*. P. 9.

X. *The Recruitment of Shock-Troop Teachers*

1. Reilly, Sister Mary Paul (O. S. B.). What must I do? Milwaukee, Bruce Publishing Co., 1950, pp. 32-33.

2. *Ibid*. P. 61.

3. *Ibid*. P. 66.

4. Poage, Rev. Godfrey (C. P.) (Paulist). Many are called. St. Paul, Catechetical Guild Educational Society, 1955, p. 13.

5. *Ibid*. P. 19.

6. *Ibid*. P. 17.

7. *Ibid*. P. 18.

8. *Ibid*. P. 23.

9. *Ibid*. Pp. 47-48.

10. Sullivan, William L. Under orders. P. 38.

11. Enchiridion Symbolorum, p. 607.

Index

Date Due

JAN 1 1 1962			
JUL 1 7 1962			
MY 27 '63			
	PRINTED	IN U. S. A.	